OVERVIEW

Overview

Do you have problem performers in your workplace? Do some of your staff members fail to deliver, or consistently arrive at work late? And whose fault is that? Do you blame them, or do you blame yourself?

Jon, Judy, David, and Tom are employees, each with different characteristics and possible problems. Are there any similarities between them and your own staff?

Jon

Jon has been over budget for the past three months. He's always on the production floor, and everyone turns to him when the machines fail. He can't plan or meet his monthly budgets, so he spends his time doing the job that he knows.

Judy

Judy was hired last fall. She was definitely the best applicant. Initially, her lack of sales experience was a problem, but she's doing better now. Her sales figures are still low, but the other salespeople like her and help her out whenever they can.

David

David is a technically gifted employee. But he never seems to finish one job - he prefers to start the next, more interesting challenge. Maybe it's just the down side of a creative personality.

Tom

Tom doesn't learn from his mistakes. His customers think he's abrupt, and they regularly complain about him. Now his annual appraisal is due, and his manager can finally talk to him about his attitude and his performance.

Unfortunately, if your employees resemble any of these people, then you are partly to blame for their problem performance.

Here's why:
- Jon is doing the wrong job.
- Judy was hired for the wrong position.
- David isn't motivated.
- Tom hasn't received feedback.

Every organization has some problem performers, but these problems can be avoided. It's an uncomfortable lesson to learn, but an organization only has itself to blame when it has to play catch-up on problem performance.

When problem performance is accepted as a normal part of the organization's existence, then a golden opportunity has been missed.

So how do you prevent problem performance?

The recipe is plain and simple:
- Choose the right people--even if your new hires do not perform well, at least you know that they have the ability.

Problem Performance Management

- Tell your employees exactly what you want them to do. If you haven't explained your standards of performance to your employees, then they will never meet your expectations.
- Tell your employees how they're doing. If you fail to give your employees feedback, eventually performance standards will drop.

Preventing poor performance isn't complicated. This course will teach you step-by-step prevention of problem performance in your organization.

*

Problem performance comes from problem performers, and they are easy to spot. They are the ones you are having problems with. That sounds easy, but this truism hides the real complexity of identifying problem performance.

This course will help you to distinguish between conduct and performance. Your response to one should be different from your response to the other. You might believe that good performance is a function of character. If so, what are the most significant attributes to look for?

And you might believe that excellent performance is developed by competition. This course will guide you through the controversial issue of forced rankings as a means of managing performance.

To manage problem performance, you will need to identify its causes to find relevant solutions. The causes may lie in the attitudes of workers, or their ability to perform. But you need to remember that your employees work in a context, and that sometimes the working system hinders good performance. This course will provide you with the information necessary to analyze the causes of problem performance in your organization.

In addition, you must be able to quantify levels of performance. You can't tell employees that they are not performing well, and then expect them to improve without quantifying and detailing that information. The last lesson in this course describes how to measure performance.

This course will enable you to identify problem performance. You will then be ready to tackle performance improvement.

**

Turning problem performance into good performance is probably the most important element of all performance management systems.

Before you can help an employee to improve her performance, you have to tell her that she has a problem. This, of course, sounds easy. But often the first step is the hardest. This course will guide you through the right way to begin.

Many managers think that their job is then finished--it's up to the worker to improve. They're wrong! This course will help you to create effective improvement plans, and to know when to use external agencies for support.

You will examine the three most useful techniques for supporting performance improvement, and by the end of the course you will be able to:

- devise an effective training plan,
- coach your workers toward improved performance,
- organize the supervisors' work so that it has the maximum impact on performance.

Problem Performance Management

Finally, you will move from improving worker performance to improving the situations they work in. This means that you can maximize their opportunities to perform well.

When you have completed this course, you'll feel confident that you have identified everything possible to help your workers improve their problem performance.

***

Effective discipline is the foundation of effective organizations. An organization has to set standards for the behavior and performance of all employees, and must maintain those standards if it is to be effective.

Managers who have to implement the disciplinary proceedings in their organizations must be clear and confident in the way that they approach this task, however uncomfortable they personally feel about it. If they are not confident, then significant problems result.

Ray

"I suspended Joe for constant swearing, and warned him that the next step was termination. But the next day, I had to call him in because we couldn't cope without him. Now I really don't know what to do."

Connie

"I called Marie to give her a written reprimand. Before I had even started, she told me that she was entitled to have someone present with her. I didn't realize that. I thought we'd all prefer to keep this sort of thing quiet."

Both Ray and Connie have mismanaged the disciplinary actions they wanted to take. Ray wasn't prepared for the implications of suspending Joe, and Connie didn't follow the correct procedures in her interview with Marie. Both have now compromised themselves for when they next need to discipline employees.

This course will ensure that you know how to prepare for, and implement disciplinary proceedings efficiently and effectively. A well-handled disciplinary event is a sign of good management.

But there are arguments about the design of the disciplinary proceedings in organizations today. Some writers argue that the conventional, progressive, and punitive approach to discipline, developed in the 1930's, is no longer appropriate for contemporary industrial relations. They argue that a more flexible system is needed; one which is without punishment at its heart. This course will provide you with both models, in enough depth for you to assess which approach is more appropriate to you.

This course will ensure that whatever system you decide upon, you can operate it effectively, with an understanding of the legal implications of what you are doing. These are essential skills for all managers.

CHAPTER 1 - *Problem Performance Prevention*

CHAPTER 1 - Problem Performance Prevention

Section 1 - Choosing the Right People
Section 2 - Performance Expectations
Section 3 - Giving Performance Feedback

Section 1 - Choosing the Right People
Section 1 - Choosing the Right People

As a manager, if you have to deal with workers who are problem performers, then you have already missed part of the opportunity to prevent poor performance. If you agree with this statement, then you can appreciate the importance of prevention in managing problem performers. And one of the most effective preventive measures is recruiting the right people from the outset.

One definition of quality is "fit for purpose." Although this term is usually applied to goods and services, it could also be applied to employee performance. Employees must be able to perform as required.

To achieve high quality employee performance, certain attributes must be present in a job's design--a job's design must follow the principle of being fit for purpose. Job design is usually identified in job descriptions and required specifications. But other factors, such as resources that make it possible for an employee to perform well also affect the design of a job.

The key to selecting the appropriate candidate is taking a consistent approach. You should have started by matching your requirements with the details of the application forms and resumes. At this stage, you can't accept vague statements. During the interview, you should have asked performance-based and probing questions to get to the heart of the candidate's experience. Then you should have used the same techniques to elicit information from a reference.

You may be skilled at selecting your employees, but the acid test is how well they actually perform. Many employers think it is sensible to extend the selection process, and they add a probationary period to evaluate the employee.

Probationary periods must be approached carefully. The consequences of poor performance during this period must be emphasized. In federal or unionized organizations, a probationary period of employment is usually built into a contract of employment, so that all sides understand the scope of probation.

Choosing the right people

Choosing the right people

As a manager, if you have to deal with workers who are problem performers, then you have already missed part of the opportunity to prevent poor performance.

If you agree with this statement, then you can appreciate the importance of prevention in managing problem performers. And one of the most effective preventive measures is recruiting the right people from the outset.

Too many people think that effective recruitment means being a good interviewer, and being able to intuit who is the right person for the job.

In fact, effective interviewing must be based on facts, not intuition. It requires preparation before conducting the interview, and evaluation of the employee after he's hired to see how well he does the job.

Problem Performance Management

Effective recruitment means that you have clearly identified the tasks and performance standards that you expect from a worker, and you have made that explicit during the interview. It is much easier to maintain high performance levels with new workers who want to impress. You can also use the probationary period as a vehicle for assessing new workers' real performance. They may not always perform well, but at least they have started well.

If you recruit effectively, you will:
- hire people who are capable of performing well from the outset,
- establish a culture of high performance in the workplace,
- state publicly the standard of work you expect.

Jenny and Ray are managers in the same organization. They have had different experiences with recruiting.

Jenny: I hired her because she reminded me of Estelle, but she's not like Estelle at all. I had some doubts about her at first, but I didn't pursue it. She didn't come to the last group meeting--she said that during the interview, I said that she could sometimes work from home. I didn't mean that she could work from home whenever she felt like it!

Ray: You don't need to tell me, I know. She's persuaded Tony, in my department, to look for any excuse to work at home. I've told him that I need to know that he's going to do the work properly before he gains that privilege, but he points to her situation as a precedent and insists on the same treatment.

Jenny failed to recruit effectively and is now paying the price. She didn't really know what she wanted from this staff member, so she can't really complain if she doesn't get it. She missed her chance in the first days after the hire to address any performance problems, and now the habits are ingrained. Jenny's lack of clarity about job expectations during the interview will come back to haunt her.

Ray has seen the impact of this hire on his team. The culture of problem performance has been strengthened by this hire, and any statement about high performance standards will have much less influence with the staff members in the future.

Question

Walter tells his managers that effective recruitment is the foundation of performance management. What statements should he use to support this point of view?

Options:

1. Effective recruitment doesn't require lengthy preparation.

2. Effective recruitment sends a clear message about the standards of work you expect.

3. Pick the right people, and you can establish a culture of high performance in the workplace.

4. Recruit effectively, and you will pick people who are capable of performing well from the outset. 5. Effective recruitment means that you have the right worker for life.

Answer

In fact, the benefits of effective recruitment are that you start with people who are capable of high performance, and you ensure that this is recognized as the normal standard. This will create a culture of high performance.

Problem Performance Management

Option 1: Incorrect. In order for recruitment to be effective, it is vital that necessary preparations be made. This will take careful consideration.

Option 2: Correct. If the company's standards are clear, people will know what to expect in the workplace. Then they will be able to decide whether or not they are willing to live up to that standard.

Option 3: Correct. A culture of high performance encourages individual employees to be high performers themselves.

Option 4: Correct. It will take employees less time to get up to speed on their responsibilities, and they will be more able to quickly meet what is expected of them.

Option 5: Incorrect. Effective recruitment is about the standard and culture of high performance that Walter expects in the company.

Choose the right people and they will perform well--choose the wrong people, and the consequences for performance will be negative. If you follow the methods outlined in this lesson, you'll be able to recruit high performers.

Job design factors that affect performance

Job design factors that affect performance

One definition of quality is "fit for purpose." Although this term is usually applied to goods and services, it could also be applied to employee performance. Employees must be able to perform as required.

To achieve high quality employee performance, certain attributes must be present in a job's design--a job's design must follow the principle of being fit for purpose. Job design is usually identified in job descriptions and required specifications. But other factors, such as resources that make it possible for an employee to perform well also affect the design of a job.

If you want effective performance, you must ensure that the elements of job design that enable good performance are available. Even the best workers can fail if they do not have the requirements to do the job. So an essential part of preventing problem performance is analyzing job design. This analysis is usually performed when preparing to hire a new employee, although job design should be regularly reviewed during appraisals. There are four elements in job design that particularly affect performance.

Skills and Knowledge

You must define the skills and knowledge you expect people to bring to the job. Failure to do this leads to problem performance. Decide what can be improved through training.

Relationships

Performance will be affected by the extent to which the job stands alone or is dependent on the performance of others. If the work is a shared process, it can be difficult to know who has contributed to the overall performance.

Outcomes

Performance is partly defined in relation to outcomes, so you must review how the measures of outcome will work. Is your standard meaningful? Ensure that the task is achievable, and that resources are available to enable good performance.

Controls

The relationship of supervisory control to performance is vital. You must identify how much direct control each worker will need to perform well. Self-control is an important motivating factor that can affect performance.

Job design must be properly identified if problem performance is to be prevented. Here are some examples of key job design elements that will enable effective performance management.

Skills and knowledge

Skill Set: Unix admin, Qualification: BE/MCA/B.tech; Experience: two to three years; Essential: must have configured DNS, NIS, NFS; Must have experience with Shell Scripting and volume managers like Veritas and Solstice.

Relationships

Reports to the finance manager. Interacts daily with sales admins. No communication with customers except by e-mail. Interacts with sales and finance to finish tasks.

Outcomes

The goal is to ensure the release of clinical batches and product reports for statutory dossiers within the planned timeframe, according to the described procedures, and within a precise budget.

Control

Independent worker who can self-manage and complete tasks. Bonus achievement system in operation.

Monthly performance reviews conducted with immediate supervisor.

Question

These are some essential job design elements for the office administrator at Pearson Brothers. Which of these elements will affect performance?

Options:

1. completes monthly statistics on absences and holidays and submits report to CEO

2. receives salary equal to point three of the pay scale for administrators

3. works in conjunction with sales manager to authorize and pay sales staff expenses

4. requires experience and certification in general office software; training in using customer contact database will be provided

5. works under daily supervision of office manager

Answer

In fact, the elements in job design that affect performance are knowledge and skills, relationships, outcomes, and control systems.

Option 1: Correct. By viewing this, prospective employees will better know what outcomes will be expected of them if they get the job.

Option 2: Incorrect. The four parts of job design include skills and knowledge, relationships, outcomes, and control. Salary, while important, is does not fit into one of these categories.

Option 3: Correct. This is the relationships part of job design. Prospective employees will know who they will be working with in order to meet the desired outcomes.

Option 4: Correct. This section of the job design outlines the skills and knowledge that are expected. It allows people investigating the position to know if their qualifications meet the requirements of the job.

Option 5: Correct. This statement clearly communicates the degree of control that the position will have. By reading this, prospective employees can know if they are willing to submit themselves to the level that is stated.

So how does job design affect performance? Job designs that are correctly and clearly defined enable performance management because they help to avoid performance problems. Conversely, failure to correctly define a job design makes problem performance more likely.

John

John was criticized for poor supervision of trainees. John was hired because of his accountant qualifications, and experience with staff supervision was not part of the selection criteria. In fact, he was told that he would mainly work alone.

Mary

Mary's team was consistently rated as the worst team in the company. But Mary's performance was among the highest. The company based bonuses on team performance, and Mary's contribution was not recognized.

Elaine

Elaine was assessed as a poor performer because her output level was lower than the other machine operators. But the measurement didn't compensate for machine downtime. Elaine used the oldest and least reliable machine.

Danny

As a new trainee, Danny was left to his own devices until a customer complained. She said that a letter she received from Danny was abrupt and discourteous. Then Danny's supervisor criticized the style of the majority of his previous letters.

John's job design did not identify staff supervision as a necessary skill, but the job included that element. It's not surprising that he did not perform well in that area because he had neither the requisite skills nor any experience. On the other hand, Mary did perform well, but the relationships element of her job design failed to identify how her individual performance would be measured against the performance of other team members.

Elaine's performance was measured by her outputs. But the measurement failed to allow for the inadequate resources that she was supposed to work with. This resulted in Elaine being incorrectly labeled as a problem performer.

As a trainee, Danny obviously required close supervision, but in fact he received very little. If the need for supervision had been properly identified, then he would not have made the mistakes he did.

Case Study: Question 1 of 2
Scenario

Eddie Butler maintained the inventory database at the Pressco warehouse. He had been recruited with no database experience but received full-time training during his probationary months. He was also able to attend a database users' meeting near his parents' home, which allowed him to visit them.

Eddie had to interact closely with Marge, the sales administrator, to meet his goal of reducing overstock by 20 percent in his first quarter. As Eddie had no experience analyzing stock, Marge had to do it for him but received no credit for this. Marge couldn't even complain to anyone as her boss had left the company last year, so she was left to alone, though she lacked confidence in staff supervision.

Analyze the job design for Eddie and Marge to determine how it impacts performance, and then answer these questions.

Question

Which statements correctly establish the way Eddie's performance would be affected by the job design?

Options:

1. If Eddie were to perform well, he should not have been recruited to this job without specific database experience.

2. The knowledge and skills training in databases given by the company allowed for a lack of previous relevant experience.

3. The bonus of the trip to see his parents would motivate Eddie toward better performance.

4. The outcome determined for Eddie would have a negative impact on performance because it would be impossible to reduce overstocks while engaging in full-time training.

Answer

In fact, Eddie's performance would be positively affected by the additional training, and negatively affected by the impossible outcome.

Option 1: Incorrect. In the job design it was determined that it would be sufficient to hire someone without the necessary database skills as long as they received proper training.

Option 2: Correct. In this case, training was determined to be sufficient to overcome any gaps between Eddie's skills and the company's expectations. The job design allowed for this flexibility.

Option 3: Incorrect. While the bonus trip might have some impact on Eddie's performance, it didn't really relate to the job and, therefore, was not a part of the job design.

Option 4: Correct. There is a conflict in the stated outcomes which will lead to dissatisfaction for Eddie due to his inability to perform that which is expected of him.

Case Study: Question 2 of 2

Which elements in Marge's job design would have an impact on her performance?

Options:

1. Marge's performance would be affected by the difficulty of establishing her contribution to the shared task with Eddie.

2. The lack of supervisory control would have a detrimental impact on Marge's performance.

3. Marge would be motivated toward higher performance by the responsibility of her supervisory relationship to Eddie.

4. Marge could not control her own work, and this would affect her performance.

Answer

In fact, Marge's performance would be affected by her lack of supervision and the failure to distinguish her contribution to the shared task with Eddie.

Option 1: Correct. This is a relationship issue that has an impact on Marge's performance. Since Marge's and Eddie's responsibilities are shared, it will be difficult to determine Marge's contribution.

Option 2: Correct. Marge was given no supervision, which resulted in her being placed in a demoralizing situation.

Option 3: Incorrect. Her relationship to Eddie was not supervisory. Consequently, it will be very difficult for her to gain recognition for her contributions.

Option 4: Incorrect. Marge could control her own work, but the lack of supervision took her work out of the larger context of the company's operations.

So Eddie's performance was affected beneficially by the design of his job because Pressco had allowed for his lack of experience with their database. However, this was contrasted with the outcome he was expected to achieve, which was unrealistic in the light of time demands. And a lack of supervision would be likely to have an adverse effect on Marge's performance. This would be compounded by a design that did not distinguish between her contribution, and Eddie's contribution, to the shared task.

Identifying job design is an essential component of performance management. Many performance problems can be avoided if you carefully examine the job requirements of your employees and whether you provide resources that will enable achievement.

By asking yourself the key questions covered in this topic, you can save a lot of time and effort. If you fail to effectively identify job design, then you will probably have to deal with problem performance.

Techniques to prevent problem performance

Techniques to prevent problem performance

Managers hire the best candidate when selecting staff members, right? Well, if they always chose effectively, then there would be far fewer problem performers.

Your selection procedures must be carefully examined to prevent problem performance. In your selection procedures, you should consider three vital questions to prevent problem performance.
- Have the candidates performed well in the past?
- Can they perform well now?
- Will they perform effectively when they are given the job?

Your selection procedure must include these questions, and ensure that they are answered.

There are three ways to find the answers to these questions.

Application forms and resumes

You need to match the job requirements that you have devised with the details from the application forms and resumes. If there are information gaps, you can address these by asking questions at the interview.

Interview Questions

During the interview, use performance-based questions, which are focused on identifying past achievements. The assumption behind this is that past behavior is a good predictor of future conduct.

References

Use references to verify the information you have gained from application forms and resumes and the interview. The last employer is usually the most significant performance reference.

Ramon and Hester are managers at Corndollies Inc. Both of them have recently recruited new workers.

Ramon: I don't think that I'm good at selecting new hires. My last hire hasn't turned out so well.

Hester: Yes, I'd heard that she wasn't performing well.

Ramon: She was so good during the interview. Positive, enthusiastic, and a really good personality. I wish I'd determined what I was looking for before I interviewed her. But she was just like Jane, and Jane was excellent at the job.

Hester: Didn't you check her qualifications and experience at the interview?

Ramon: I thought I had, but when I look back on it, I see that my questions weren't really focused.

Hester: But didn't her application form list her experience?

Ramon: I didn't really read it. She interviewed so well...

Hester: Let me guess. You didn't call for references either. Well, you certainly have nobody but yourself to blame.

Ramon has made some typical errors, and he will now have to work so much harder to get a good performance out of his new hire. He didn't find any evidence to match his job requirements because he didn't identify what he wanted.

So with nothing to focus on, Ramon based his judgment on the way the candidate presented herself at the interview. Unfortunately, her job description did not involve attending interviews!

Question

Jeremy is preparing to hire a new assistant for his team. He carefully examines his procedure to ensure that he does everything he can to hire the best candidate. Match each selection procedure element to the appropriate corresponding comment.

Options:

A. application forms and resumes
B. interview questions
C. references

Targets:

1. performance-based questioning
2. preferably from last employer
3. match with job requirements

Answer

An effective selection procedure involves matching application forms and resumes with the job requirements, using performance-based questioning at the interview, and getting references from a previous employer.

By asking performance-based questions, Jeremy can examine the candidate's past experience, which should be a good predictor of his future behavior.

The most recent employer will be able to give the most current account of the candidate's behavior. Jeremy should be able to contact the references and get a good idea of the kind of employee the candidate really is.

Jeremy can compare the information that the candidate provides with the job requirements he has already identified. If there are gaps, he can discuss those topics in an interview.

So, which techniques should you use during each part of the selection procedure to ensure that you choose the candidate who will perform the best?

Application Forms and Resumes

Create a job description, list performance requirements, and rate the importance of these. Then sift through the resumes and application forms to cross-reference this information. It's easier if you design the application form to support this process.

Interview Questions

Performance-based questions help you gather specific evidence. Ask a question like, "Tell me about a time when..." and continue with probing questions that investigate the detail provided in the opening response. Avoid yes or no answers.

References

Try to get telephone references. Have specific performance-based questions ready, and don't forget to probe. You want evidence of performance, not general platitudes.

Problem Performance Management

Some employers may be reluctant to give a full reference for one of their past employees for fear of potential lawsuits. They may only provide factual information such as dates of employment. But don't let this put you off. In their book, "Dealing with Problem Employees--a Legal Guide," Amy DelPro and Lisa Guerin cite research stating that up to 90 percent of employers ask for, and check, an applicant's references.

Now prepare to hire an administrative assistant in your organization. You will need to study the job description and review Henry Pool's resume.

Question

Some elements from the job description are listed here along with some notes based on Henry's resume. Match each element of the job description to the relevant note from Henry's resume.

Options:

A. international/intercultural exchange experience

B. computer literate

C. educational achievements

D. cross-cultural experience

Targets:

1. proficient in Lotus 1-2-3, MS Access, and other software

2. no evidence

3. administrative support to a charity organizing educational visits to Europe

4. B.S. in business management

Answer

Actually, based on his application, Henry does not seem to have cross-cultural experience.

These skills indicate that Henry Pool fills the requirement to be computer literate.

Nothing on Henry's application indicates that he has cross-cultural experience.

Henry's experience with this charity will have given him the international/intercultural exchange experience he needs for this job.

By indicating that he has a Bachelor of Science degree in business management, Henry makes it clear what his educational achievements are.

Now you are going to interview Henry Pool.

You need to use performance-based questions to establish concrete evidence of past performance that is relevant to the job requirements that you have specified.

Don't forget to ask probing questions to verify the details of Henry's past performance. Probing questions often follow the who, what, when, and how pattern. They do not need to be accusatory or aggressive, but you want to verify Henry's past performance.

With performance-based and probing questions, it was possible to establish a good range of evidence about things that Henry has done in the past, and therefore should be able to do in the position he has applied for.

Now, if you wish to give the position to Henry, you should check his references, preferably through a telephone call with his previous or most relevant employer.

Here's how Mary from human resources checks Henry's references with his last employer, Angela Simms.

Mary: Henry has applied for a position that requires computer literacy.

Problem Performance Management

Angela: Oh, Henry is really good with computers. He certainly was proficient with all of our software, and that includes the normal range of small office applications.

Mary: We need someone with good written communication skills. Can you recall how Henry presented written information?

Angela: Oh, he did well. He was really good at communicating with e-mails. Mary: What about more formal methods? Did he write letters for you?

Angela: No, I usually did that.

Mary: Was writing letters part of his duties?

Angela: Well, yes, but I wasn't entirely happy with his style. He didn't follow a standard business letter format, and I'm a bit of a stickler for that.

The reference check substantiates some of Henry's abilities, but it casts doubt on an important performance criterion. Now that you have all the data, you can make a decision about Henry's suitability for the position.

Case Study: Question 1 of 3
Scenario

You are trying to select a candidate for the position of inside sales representative.

You will consider the candidates' applications and resumes and then interview them. Finally, you will call their last employers for references.

Answer these three questions, in order, to show how you will avoid hiring a problem performer.

Question

The job description for the position of inside sales representative identifies the following requirements: six months experience cold-calling, successful closure of new corporate client accounts, and outbound call quota averaging 50 calls each day.

Which items, taken from an application form, match these requirements?

Options:

1. 1998-2000 Acme Double Glazing. Outside sales representative. Followed up with documentation.

2. Prospected potential clients, contacted decision makers, and closed new business.

3. Novamoro Corporation Feb 2000 - Jun 2001. Inside sales representative. Generated fresh leads and exceeded minimum call quota of 60 outbound calls per day, averaging between 80 and 120 outbound cold calls.

4. Generated fresh leads from cold calls to proper channels for immediate response/resolution.

Answer

In fact, the application form item "Prospected potential clients, contacted decision makers, and closed new business," and the applicant's work at Novamoro Corporation match the job description's requirements.

Option 1: Incorrect. Information such as this, although valid, does not directly match up against the job description, and should not be considered in this comparison.

Option 2: Correct. This information in the candidate's application matches with the portion of the job description that reads, "successful closure of new corporate client accounts."

Option 3: Correct. If the candidate's claims are accurate, they should be able to meet the job description's smaller quota of only 50 outbound calls per day.

Option 4: Incorrect. This information was not addressed in the job description and cannot be directly matched to it.

Case Study: Question 2 of 3

You are now going to interview a candidate. You want to establish that she has generated significant sales from inactive customers.

Which interview questions would most help you to determine the evidence for this requirement?

Options:

1. What techniques do you have to reactivate existing customers?
2. Can you tell me about a time when you reactivated an existing customer?
3. So what volume of sales did this customer bring in?
4. How did you deal with old customers who were angry at being contacted again?

Answer

You need to use both a performance-based and a probing question, which together establish the evidence for the requirement.

Option 1: Incorrect. This question focuses on the candidate's techniques, but doesn't address their past performance. A performance oriented question focuses on what the candidate has actually done and the effect that their efforts had.

Option 2: Correct. This is an example of a performance oriented question. It focuses the candidate on past achievements that relate to the future requirements of the job.

Option 3: Correct. This gives you measurable information that you can compare to the job description.

You can use this information to make predictions concerning the candidates potential for success.

Option 4: Incorrect. This is not an example of a performance oriented question. Performance oriented questions will require the candidate to quantify ways in which their past performance impacted their company.

Case Study: Question 3 of 3

You are considering hiring Ian Hargreaves for the position of inside sales representative. He has said that he is computer literate and a team player.

When you call his last employer for a reference, what questions will you ask to verify Ian's claims?

Options:

1. Can you tell me about Ian's work as a member of a team?
2. Would you describe Ian as computer literate?
3. Can you give me a specific example of Ian's computer literacy capabilities?
4. So, is Ian a real whiz kid with computers?

Answer

Actually, you need to use performance-based and probing questions to get evidence to verify Ian's assertions.

Option 1: Correct. This question probes Ian's last employer concerning Ian's past work as well as his ability to work within a team.

Option 2: Incorrect. This question doesn't verify Ian's computer capabilities in a quantifiable way. Option 3: Correct. This is a performance based question that requires Ian's previous employer to
specifically cite examples of Ian's past performance.

Option 4: Incorrect. In order to be performance based, this question should be rephrased to ask the employer to identify past examples. You can use that information to make future predictions about Ian's performance.

The key to selecting the appropriate candidate is taking a consistent approach. You should have started by matching your requirements with the details of the application forms and resumes. At this stage, you can't accept vague statements. During the interview, you should have asked performance-based and probing questions to get to the heart of the candidate's experience. Then you should have used the same techniques to elicit information from a reference.

Selecting the right people is an absolute must if you want to prevent problem performance. There is no guarantee that a candidate won't perform poorly at some time in his career with you, but at least you will know his capabilities.

Probationary periods

You may be skilled at selecting your employees, but the acid test is how well they actually perform. Many employers think it is sensible to extend the selection process, and they add a probationary period to evaluate the employee.

Probationary periods must be approached carefully. The consequences of poor performance during this period must be emphasized. In federal or unionized organizations, a probationary period of employment is usually built into a contract of employment, so that all sides understand the scope of probation.

But even for employment "at will," in which there is no contract, it is sensible to establish standards for probationary workers. These standards should be applied consistently to avoid challenges based on unjust termination of employment.

Problem Performance Management

During the probationary period, which usually lasts 60 or 90 days, the employee's performance is rigorously evaluated. If you consider the probationary period as an extension of the selection process for a new employee, then this helps to identify two significant characteristics of effective probation.

Employee

A new employee rapidly absorbs the attitudes and culture of an organization. It is difficult to change these impressions later.

Employer

An employer must see the probationary period as a time not only to assess new workers, but also to support them and build their skills.

When Rufus hired Stella to work at Omnitrade, they discussed what the probationary period meant to them.

Rufus: We have a contracted probationary period of 60 days. This gives us a chance to see what you can do. But we also use the probationary period to make sure that you have all the skills that you need to perform as effectively as possible. And you can learn how we do things around here. We have an excellent orientation program.

Stella: Great, I definitely want to learn the Omnitrade way. I'm really interested to see how you apply the CRP software. I'm not entirely familiar with it.

Rufus: Don't worry. I know that's new to you, so you'll be given full training on it as soon as you start. We understand that it'll take a while for you to get up to speed.

Rufus is going to use the probationary period to introduce Stella to the Omnitrade philosophy. Rufus will also ensure that Stella knows how to use the CRP software before he assesses her performance.

Question

Travelrite has a 90-day probationary period for all new employees. What are the characteristics of an effective probationary period?

Options:

1. Probation should include an orientation period to explain the culture of Travelrite.

2. Probation can only be included as part of a written contract.

3. Probation can only occur in unionized and federal organizations.

4. Skills training needs to be available to ensure that all new employees can perform as well as possible.

Answer

Actually, an effective probationary period needs to have an element of skills support, and an introduction to the culture and ethos of the company.

Option 1: Correct. The orientation will help Travelrite's new employees to be more familiar with how they fit in their new environment.

Option 2: Incorrect. The employment contract doesn't contribute to the effectiveness of the probationary period because the probationary period is all about orientating and training the new Travelrite employees.

Option 3: Incorrect. An effective probationary period consists of orientating Travelrite's new employees, as well as ensuring they have the skills they need to perform. The type of company doesn't relate to effective probation periods.

Option 4: Correct. If Travelrite's new employees don't have the necessary skills to perform the job, they will be less likely to have a successful probation period.

So how can you make the probationary period an effective way to prevent problem performance? You will have to take actions focused on both the employee and the employer.

Role Model

You must provide new hires with a supportive role model. Experience is not everything, and attitude really counts when supporting a new hire. Don't choose a person with a negative attitude, or someone who doesn't conform to company policies.

Feedback

Give formal feedback to your new employee. Probation should reinforce the culture of performance appraisal to the employee, and doing so at this early stage is very influential on subsequent behavior.

Development Plan

You should devise a program for development. Use the information obtained from the candidate during the interview, and match it against the performance requirements. You should include the development program in conditions for employment.

Extensions

Be prepared to extend the probationary period with a formal agreement. This situation may occur if you find that performance is not good enough, but you feel that it can be improved in a cost effective manner, or if the employee incurred unavoidable absences.

Case Study: Question 1 of 3
Scenario

You are a manager responsible for organizing the probationary period for Will, a new staff member in your organization.

Will has been hired to work as an assistant accountant in the purchasing department. He is qualified for the position, but he has limited experience supporting managers with budgetary oversight.

Answer these questions, in order, to use the probationary period to prevent problem performance.

Question

Will is on Mike's team, and he has suggested that Will be mentored by Colin, Arthur, or May. From the descriptions of these people, select the best person to mentor Will.

Options:

1. Colin is an experienced worker. He has a high performance level and is always rated "excellent" by his supervisor. But Colin is very busy, and he would have to drop some work to support Will.

2. Arthur is the fastest worker in the department. He is renowned for completing tasks ahead of time, and has developed unofficial shortcuts to maintain this reputation. He has mentored other new hires and enjoys showing them the quickest ways to do things.

3. May is a very conscientious employee who insists on painstaking accuracy. She sets high standards, and has refused to work with colleagues who are willing to sign off on accounts that meet company guidelines but do not meet May's exacting standards.

Answer

Problem Performance Management

In fact, Colin would be the best role model. Arthur does not perform to company standards, and May's attitude is counterproductive.

Option 1: Correct. Colin performs up to the company's standards and does so in the way the company wants them done. His mentoring will help Will to learn similar behaviors.

Option 2: Incorrect. Arthur is productive, but he doesn't adhere to the company's way of doing things. This resistance will likely be passed on to Will if Arthur is made the mentor.

Option 3: Incorrect. Having May be Will's mentor would likely result in Will learning all about May's standard, rather than the company's.

Case Study: Question 2 of 3

Mike suggests a number of plans for the interactions between Colin and Will.

Which would be the most appropriate suggestion?

Options:

1. "I expect that Colin will give Will all the support and feedback he needs on a day-to-day basis. He can do this while they go through the accounts together."

2. "I suggest an introductory meeting, and then another meeting in the last week of the probationary period. I don't think it's sensible to plan anything apart from that."

3. "Will and Colin should meet weekly throughout the probationary period. I think the meetings should be planned in advance and records should be kept."

Answer

Actually, regular, formal feedback is essential in the probationary period.

Option 1: Incorrect. Will needs an organized and formal time set aside to discuss issues pertaining to his performance. Fitting it on top of another responsibility will not give the meeting the emphasis that it needs.

Option 2: Incorrect. Will needs feedback on a regular basis. Otherwise, he will be unable to make adjustments to his behavior as he proceeds through the probationary period.

Option 3: Correct. Applicable feedback is vital to Will's success in the company. With it, he can know areas where he is doing well, as well as areas in which he needs to improve.

Case Study: Question 3 of 3

Will has limited experience supporting managers with budgetary oversight. How should you respond to this in the probationary period?

Options:

1. "If we get the chance, we'll enroll him in a training course about supporting managers with budgets."

2. "There are no relevant training opportunities for Will to learn how to support managers. So I will extend his probation until he's had budgetary oversight training."

3. "If he's OK with everything else, then I can assume that he is capable of supporting managers."

4. "At the interview, I identified Will's lack of experience in supporting managers. So it's vital that he is given the support to develop that skill. Then he can practice during the probationary period and be assessed on his performance."

Answer

Problem Performance Management

In fact, Will needs the support to perform well, and if it is not forthcoming, then you should think about extending the probationary period.

Option 1: Incorrect. Will's success should not be left to chance. Will's probation should be extended until there is a relevant training opportunity.

Option 2: Correct. You can use training programs to bridge gaps in Will's abilities. If no applicable course is found, it is appropriate to extend the probation period until a proper alternative is identified.

Option 3: Incorrect. An assumption such as this is taking the risk that Will will be unable to perform the required skills on his own. In order to obtain the performance from him that you desire, you need to enable him with the tools he needs.

Option 4: Correct. You must enable Will to do the job by giving him proper support in areas where he might need extra help.

Will needs to be mentored by someone who has a positive attitude and works within company standards. Although Arthur works quickly, he uses unofficial shortcuts, so he isn't an appropriate role model. May's exacting standards may hinder Will, rather than help him, so Colin is by far the best role model. Will and Colin should meet regularly so that Will can adjust to a formal appraisal system and get regular feedback.

When you consider Will's training needs, you must think back to the interview. It is important to devise a plan that will address his needs. If necessary, you may have to extend the probationary period to ensure that he has ample opportunity to gain the skills he needs.

Sorin Dumitrascu

Probation is a cost-effective screening and development mechanism to prevent problem performance in your workplace. So use it well, and appoint workers who will succeed.

Section 2 - Performance Expectations

Section 2 - Performance Expectations

Managers cannot manage without assuming a standard of performance to measure workers against. But this must be communicated to improve performance. Criticism and praise aren't meaningful if they are not based on a known and realistic expectation.

All of these driving forces rely on the motivating force of goals, and for goals to be motivational, they must be:
- challenging, but attainable,
- specific, not vague.

This approach is called goal setting theory. It is the basis for the management by objectives (MBO) philosophy, which attempts to cascade goals down through an organization, so that even the lowest-ranking worker can see how his or her effort supports the greater good. Specific performance objectives are created for workers to help them achieve their individual goals, which helps to achieve the organization's goals. In this approach, an individual must have precise, achievable goals to aspire to.

By observing his team members individually and looking at workflow, Barry Humphries is setting effective performance standards. But he should also try to explain to his team members how they fit into the organization, and he should set achievable goals. Sylvia ties her standards to organizational goals, and works with employees and supervisors; however, she should consider talking to customers about their expectations of people in specific positions. Sylvia should also refrain from trying to make each job role self-contained.

Communicating performance standards is an essential part of preventing problem performance. If the workers tell you that they don't know what standards are expected of them, then review your communications right now!

Establishing and communicating performance

expectations

Establishing and communicating performance expectations

Many workers can recount an experience of inadequate, incomprehensible, or nonexistent statements regarding the expectations of their performance.

Rudi: When I started, my boss said that he might not always tell me when I was doing things right, but he'd definitely tell me when I was doing things wrong. He's never said anything to me about my performance, so I suppose I'm doing things right!

Stan: My boss told me that my performance would have to be above average. But when I asked her what the average was, she didn't answer.

Carl: I was told that I'd be measured against the differentiated norms for my cohort. I never did understand what that meant!

Inez: My boss always says, "well done, that's great." But she says it to everybody, so I ignore her stupid comments.

Rudi, Inez, Stan, and Carl are now resigned to this state of affairs. But in the past, they were probably angry at the pointlessness of their performance expectations, particularly if they were penalized for not meeting them. Ineffective performance expectations are demotivating. Most people try to do the best job they can, and need to measure themselves against some form of standard. Many people rely on their own personal standards, but without external confirmation, these can be misleading.

Managers cannot manage without assuming a standard of performance to measure workers against. But this must be communicated to improve performance. Criticism and praise aren't meaningful if they are not based on a known and realistic expectation.

If you are effective at establishing and communicating performance expectations to your employees, you will reap the benefits because:

- you provide a standard against which employees can measure their performance,
- you can legitimately challenge poor performance,
- you can provide meaningful praise to employees.

"But you never told me that you expected that!" Does that sound familiar?

One obvious and common cause of problems with performance lies in the clarity and comprehension of performance expectations.

Problem Performance Management

You have to know what you expect from your staff and make sure that they know and understand this expectation, or you are leaving performance to chance.

Clearly defining and communicating your performance expectations won't automatically improve performance. But it is an absolutely necessary step along the way.

Question

Cindy is convinced that there would be real benefits if her manager would define and communicate the standards of performance that he expects from her and her colleagues. What are those benefits?

Options:

1. Performance would automatically improve.

2. Employees would be able to measure their own improvements.

3. The manager could legitimately criticize poor performance.

4. Praise from the manager would be accepted as a real reward.

Answer

In fact, when performance expectations are effectively set and communicated, employees are informed, and managers are able to legitimately praise and criticize performance.

Option 1: Incorrect. Proper communication doesn't guarantee that performance will improve. However, the employee's accountability for their performance will increase.

Option 2: Correct. Cindy and her colleagues would benefit in this way because they would have a standard upon which to judge their own performance.

Option 3: Correct. In the case of poor performers, the manager must ensure fairness by knowing that the employees know what is expected of them. If that is not the case, the manager's criticisms are compromised.

Option 4: Correct. Managers who have communicated the performance standards they expect will also be able to make judgments based on those standards. When they see cause for reward, that reward will be justified.

If you want to improve performance, you need to know what good performance is. Your employees must understand your expectations as well.

How motivation is affected by goals

How motivation is affected by goals

What motivates you to perform well at work? Do you work hard because you must, to do your job effectively? Do you enjoy feeling a sense of achievement at the end of the day?

All of these driving forces rely on the motivating force of goals, and for goals to be motivational, they must be:
- challenging, but attainable,
- specific, not vague.

This approach is called goal setting theory. It is the basis for the management by objectives (**MBO**) philosophy, which attempts to cascade goals down through an organization, so that even the lowest-ranking worker can see how his or her effort supports the greater good. Specific performance objectives are created for workers to help them achieve their individual goals, which helps to achieve the organization's goals. In this approach, an individual must have precise, achievable goals to aspire to.

MBO goals must be mutually set by the manager and the worker. However, in terms of motivation, the characteristics of attainability and specificity are more important. Managers must understand these characteristics if goals are to be used to manage workplace performance.

Attainability

A goal can't be too easy to achieve or too difficult. Motivation decreases if a task is undemanding. But a goal that is too hard to achieve is frustrating, and may be perceived as pointless, causing motivation to decline.

Specificity

Vague goals that do not describe a measured outcome are less influential than specific goals. Motivation levels are increased by the clarity of expectations, and significantly increased when results are measurable.

Your expectations of your staff members must be communicated clearly and precisely. Effective goals lead to higher performance, ineffective ones lead to problem performance.

Luanne and Oscar are two employees. See each employee to discover how expectations affected their performance.

Luanne

"Our goal was based on three employees. When Terri was sick, our boss suggested that we revise it, but we knew we could still do it. It felt great when we did."

Oscar

Problem Performance Management

"The 12 calls a day were just within our grasp. We did three at a time, and took a break after each one. That made the work manageable."

Question

Matthew believes that he's motivated his team members because he's clearly communicated his goals for them. Which goals would motivate staff members toward high performance?

Options:

1. a goal agreed on by manager and worker
2. a goal that states, "do better than last week"
3. a goal to improve sales by 15 percent over last quarter
4. a simple goal that enables team members to feel that they have achieved something immediately
5. a goal that challenges, but is manageable

Answer

In fact, goals need to be challenging but attainable, and they also need to be specific to motivate performance.

Option 1: Correct. By agreeing on it, both the manager and the worker have an investment in doing all they can to attain the goal.

Option 2: Incorrect. This goal is not specific because "last week's" results are not defined. Also, it does not state how much better the performance is expected to be.

Option 3: Correct. This is an example of a specific goal. This specificity makes it easy to know when the goal is reached.

Option 4: Incorrect. A goal must be both challenging and attainable. This particular goal is not challenging.

Option 5: Correct. If the goal is too easy, Matthew's workers could feel demeaned, resulting in poor motivation. If the goal is too hard, a sense of frustration and futility could develop, also leading to low levels of motivation.

Choose your goals carefully if you want your staff members to perform well. Everyone performs better when they can see the target in front of them.

Effective performance standards

Effective performance standards

Standards are at the heart of any consideration about managing performance in the workplace. Without defining standards for performance, managers cannot evaluate, and workers cannot improve.

For standards to be of any value in managing performance, they must have certain characteristics. If they aren't job-related, organization-wide, and accomplishment-based, then the standards are irrelevant, inappropriately focused, and without purpose.

Job-related

Avoid the temptation to relate performance standards to the person, rather than to the task. If standards are based on the person, then they become descriptive, rather than aspirational. It is impossible to compare performance between employees when descriptive standards are used.

Accomplishments

A common error is to focus on activities, and not on accomplishments. Accomplishments are outputs, but activities are the actions that produce results. "Files that are orderly and complete" is an output with qualitative or quantitative measurements. "Filing documents" is an activity.

Organization-wide

Whenever possible, link standards to organizational goals. The standards will be meaningful and valuable to the organization and to the employee. A standard of orderly and complete files relates to responding to customers within one day, because the files are up to date and accessible.

All performance standards relate to a job, not a person. They are based on accomplishments, not activities, and have an organization-wide focus.

Help Desk Assistant

- asks questions in accordance with prescribed format
- solutions don't cause other problems
- machine downtime minimized

Customer Service Supervisor

- all employees trained in use of CPR system
- 15 customer service representative calls monitored daily
- no customer dissatisfaction responses

Logistics Clerk

- vehicle itinerary devised and input on previous working day
- dispatched vehicles minimum of 75 percent of full load
- discounts offered to returning customers

Software Trainer

Problem Performance Management

- pre-course requirements issued one week prior to start
- 75 percent of courses achieve maximum rating
- follow-up courses recommended

Question

The performance standards for Paula's job as health and safety officer are written effectively.

Which characteristics do they display?

Options:

1. They identify activities, not outputs.
2. They relate to Paula's job, not to Paula as an individual.
3. They relate to Paula as an individual.
4. They identify outputs, not activities.
5. They are linked to organizational goals.

Answer

In fact, effective standards are focused on outputs, are job-related, and link to organizational objectives.

Option 1: Incorrect. The standards need to outline what is expected in Paula's company. Focusing on the activities is focusing on the path, rather than the destination.

Option 2: Correct. If the standards related to Paula as an individual, they would be descriptive and could not be compared with the performance of any other employee.

Option 3: Incorrect. If the standards focus on Paula, they will provide a point for all the employees to judge themselves. The standards must address the entire organization as well as the individual.

Option 4: Correct. These goals focus on the results, not the actions that produce them.

Option 5: Correct. This way the standards will be meaningful to the organization and the individual employees will be able to see how they fit in the larger picture.

Managers play a key role in defining, setting, and applying performance standards in relation to their employees. Job descriptions are often devised by them, or based on the information they provide, and they are in the forefront of any appraisal system. So what do you need to do to ensure that you devise effective performance standards?

Job related

You must conduct a rigorous job analysis by observing the person doing the job. This will enable you to establish how he or she completes tasks. You should also interview the employee and any other relevant person, such as a supervisor.

Accomplishments

Use a customer-focused approach that identifies the customer, and determines her expectations of that position. Or use the work flow model, which identifies the outcome of an individual job that is necessary for the next part of the task to be completed.

Organization wide

Identify cascading goals in the organization. The organizational goals must be identified, then the ones that relate specifically to the job must be isolated, and then the way that they support the achievement of this goal must be determined.

Managers like Raymond, Jackie, and Art have been effective in defining the performance standards for their teams for a number of years.

Art: I review each job annually. I target a worker, and spend as much time as I can working next to him. I get to

Problem Performance Management

know him, and the way that he does his job. That gives me a preliminary specification, which I then discuss with the supervisor and the employee. By combining these three perspectives, I completely understand the job.

Jackie: I follow up on my team's customers, both internal and external, and ask how they were treated. In my experience, customers give accurate assessments, but you need to balance the negative comments by examining the particular circumstances.

Raymond: Too many standards are meaningless to the worker. I believe that the workers have to see how their jobs matter. Then, however trivial the job is, it has a purpose. I use the mission statement and relate everything to it. So cleaning the restrooms every three hours is all about providing world-class customer care.

These managers have gone the extra mile to define performance standards because they know that the payoff is worth it. Art doesn't only rely on one source of information. He tries to get as many perspectives as possible--that way he has real data to work with. Jackie isn't afraid to check up on her staff members. She knows that the recipients of the service are the best judges of whether it is adequate.

Raymond knows that people perform better when they know why they have to. By using the mission statement, he acts as an interpreter for his team members. He explains their jobs in a way that is meaningful, and everyone on his team knows his or her place in the big picture.

Put these techniques together, and you have the recipe for defining performance standards in your workplace.

Case Study: Question 1 of 2

Scenario

Westcomb Alternatives has excellent teams, and teams that don't seem to perform so well.

Jack Bright, the CEO, asks you to compare the teams and identify what is causing the difference in performance. You decide to do this by interviewing the team leaders.

Answer these questions to identify effective performance standards.

Question

You begin with Barry Humphries' team. During the interview, Barry offers the following statements about how he sets performance standards for his team. Which statements indicate that effective performance standards have been set?

Options:

1. "I've spent time observing my team members at work, so I know what performance levels they are capable of."

2. "I won't accept any excuses for poor performance."

3. "I'm always pushing them. I set standards of performance that my staff members say can't be achieved."

4. "I look carefully at the work flow in the team, so I know if one worker can't perform well because of somebody else's tardiness."

5. "I don't confuse the team members by explaining how their jobs fit into the big picture. I just tell them to get going."

Answer

Problem Performance Management

Actually, effective performance standards are based on detailed job analysis through observing and identifying the impact of work flow on accomplishments.

Option 1: Correct. Barry Humphries knows his workers and the requirements of their jobs. He can use this knowledge to establish his expectations of his team.

Option 2: Incorrect. This statement does not account for potential disruptions to the workflow of Barry's team. Barry must know what the jobs in his team require as well what contributes to the team's accomplishments.

Option 3: Incorrect. In this case, Barry is not understanding the nature and requirements of the individual jobs within his team. This will lead to frustrated and unmotivated employees.

Option 4: Correct. By examining the work flow carefully, Barry will know not only how the team works when operating efficiently, but also when it is disrupted in some way.

Option 5: Incorrect. If the team members don't know how their job fits into the larger picture, they will not have a sense of contribution and their motivation will suffer. Barry must know their jobs and understand their accomplishments.

Case Study: Question 2 of 2

You interview Sylvia, the leader of the IT team.

Which statements indicate that effective performance standards have been set?

Options:

1. "I review my performance expectations with the employee and supervisor to determine whether they are realistic."

2. "I align each job with organizational goals."

3. "I encourage each employee to be self-reliant so they don't depend on other employees' performance."

4. "Customers are the worst source of information about performance. They don't understand technical problems."

Answer

Actually, to set effective performance standards, Sylvia has balanced her own observations of performance, and ensured that the standard is linked to the organizational goals.

Option 1: Correct. Sylvia has combined her own expectations of the team's jobs with those of team members. This gives her a balanced outlook on the standards she has set.

Option 2: Correct. Aligning each job with the organization gives the team members a sense of place within the organization. The team will feel like a part of a larger structure, providing them with higher levels of motivation.

Option 3: Incorrect. Under this statement, team members would not be understanding their jobs within the larger context of the entire company. They are less likely to feel valued, and their motivation will suffer.

Option 4: Incorrect. Customers can give valuable information about employees' performance, but Sylvia needs to balance the negative comments by looking at the particulars of each situation.

By observing his team members individually and looking at workflow, Barry Humphries is setting effective performance standards. But he should also try to explain to his team members how they fit into the organization, and he should set achievable goals. Sylvia ties her standards to organizational goals, and works with employees and supervisors; however, she should consider talking to customers about their expectations of people in specific positions. Sylvia should also refrain from trying to make each job role self-contained.

To manage performance in your team, you must consider the way that you define standards of performance. Review the way you define your standards, and adjust them to ensure results.

Effective communication of performance standards

Effective communication of performance standards

Jack has been working at Preston Fastenings as a dispatcher for years. He takes real pride in his work, and he knows from favorable comments that his customers think highly of him.

Jack's new boss, Mac, wants to have a word with him.

Mac: Jack, did you know that you are the slowest dispatcher in the company? Why are you the only dispatcher who sends written order confirmations? Nobody else does it. It's time consuming, costly, and unnecessary.

Jack: That's the way I've always done it. That's what I was taught when I started, and I think it's the right way to treat customers.

Mac: Maybe, but our policy is not to send out confirmations.

Problem Performance Management

Jack: Listen. What people do in other offices is not my concern. Nobody told me to do it any differently, and nobody has complained about it before.

Mac: Well, Jack, now I'm telling you. Don't send out confirmations anymore.

Jack: But what about the customer reactions? If they complain, you'll say I'm not doing my job properly.

Mac: No, Jack, we won't. It's the speed of your work that we are most concerned about right now. You need to get up to speed like everyone else.

Jack thinks he's doing a good job because the customers tell him he is. But his company has evaluated him on a different set of criteria. For Jack to perform well, he has to know what performance standards are expected of him.

Standards must be communicated effectively. This means considering two factors.

Methods used to communicate the standards

These methods are operational manuals, job aids, and performance guidelines. The level of complexity of the task affects the method. Simple technical jobs are more likely to have brief job aids, and more complex tasks are likely to be less directly supported with operational manuals.

Timing of the communication

You should establish the standards when you conduct an interview, and reinforce them in detail as soon as the employee is hired. You can do this during orientation, and throughout the probationary period. Standards must be reinforced during formal appraisal exercises.

Effective communication of performance standards requires appropriate methods. The standards must be applicable to the particular job. The worker should receive the information at appropriate points, and the information should be regularly reinforced.

Job Aid

X-Ray Shutdown Procedure

1. Push black button OFF.
2. Turn main switch to COOL DOWN.
3. Turn power control button OFF.
4. Wait for five minutes.
5. Remove main key

Performance Guidelines

Establish team expectations,

Adhere to CSFSC/HP policy currently in place when establishing expectations, agree to standard expectations for all members, publish and make expectations readily available for all members, make changes when necessary.

Orientation

Orientation program for a medium-size bank:

Detailed policies and procedures session includes performance review process (purpose, frequency, measurement factors, correlation with standards of performance, salary increases).

Appraisal

From a major engineering corporation: notes on completing a performance review.

From the previous review document, identify results achieved.

Assess individual performance against results required.

For the relatively simple mechanical task of the X-ray shutdown procedure, a job aid is sufficient to communicate the performance standards required. Setting performance standards for a team leader to establish team expectations requires a less specific guideline. The bank tells its new employees as part of their orientation exactly what is expected of them, and the engineering company has ensured that performance standards are constantly reinforced in its performance review procedure.

Question

Jim is a manager at Sunrise Productions. He has been tasked with ensuring the effectiveness of communicating performance standards.

Which areas should he focus on?

Options:

1. making sure that the appraisal systems in the company reinforce and update performance standards

2. ensuring that customer feedback is given to all employees

3. providing job aids to the screen print operators

4. including information about performance standards in the company orientation program

5. giving team managers performance guidelines on delivering team briefings 6. distributing the company stock market performance statistics to all divisions

Answer

In fact, effective communication of performance standards requires using the appraisal and orientation system, as well as providing appropriate job aids and performance guidelines.

Option 1: Correct. When the appraisal systems match the company standards, employees will be taught what is expected of them and how those behaviors relate to the company at large.

Option 2: Incorrect. The company sets and disseminates the standards that are to be communicated.

These can be influenced by factors such as customer feedback, but that feedback doesn't set the standard.

Option 3: Correct. The provision of a job aid for simple technical tasks is an appropriate way to communicate the desired standard.

Option 4: Correct. By timing the communication standards at the beginning of a worker's employment, Sunrise Productions can be assured that the workers know what is expected of them from the very beginning.

Option 5: Correct. Delivering performance guidelines to managers allows the managers to communicate their related expectations back to the people they manage. In this way, a consistent standard can be championed.

Option 6: Incorrect. Sunrise Productions' stock market performance is different from their standards. Communicating their standards should be done using appropriate means and timing.

Communicating performance standards is an essential part of preventing problem performance. If the workers tell you that they don't know what standards are expected of them, then review your communications right now!

Section 3 - Giving Performance Feedback

Which statements do you think are true?
- Managers are good at praising their staff members.
- Managers are good at criticizing their staff members.
- Managers are not good at praising or criticizing their staff members.

All three statements can be true in particular circumstances, but in general, many managers neither praise nor criticize their staff members effectively. In other words, they shy away from giving their staff members feedback. Why do some managers avoid this essential part of their role?

Providing feedback is a vital skill for any manager to master. But too often, feedback is poorly used and misunderstood. When this happens, feedback can backfire on the person giving, and the person receiving the feedback.

Managers do not have to force effective feedback on employees. Many managers imagine that because feedback is sometimes uncomfortable, their workers do not want or need it. This is entirely wrong. Employees want effective feedback.

Imagine a situation without feedback--for example, golfing in the dark. You don't know where the hole is or whether you hit the golf ball near it. You will quickly lose interest in the task. There is no point to it. So feedback on performance is something that most employees seek. But it has to be effective feedback, and you must use certain techniques in giving feedback to your employees to ensure that it is effective.

In the Harvard Business Review article, "A Better Way to Deliver Bad News," Jean-Francois Manzoni pointed out that many managers find giving feedback difficult. He also analyzed the common mistakes that they make.

Manzoni argues that the problem for managers stems from the framing of the situation and that this approach subsequently causes other problems. By "framing," Manzoni means the way that managers define the boundaries of the situation that they face.

Giving effective performance feedback to employees

Giving effective performance feedback to employees

Which statements do you think are true?
- Managers are good at praising their staff members.
- Managers are good at criticizing their staff members.
- Managers are not good at praising or criticizing their staff members.

All three statements can be true in particular circumstances, but in general, many managers neither praise nor criticize their staff members effectively. In other words, they shy away from giving their staff members feedback. Why do some managers avoid this essential part of their role?

Lorraine

"I think feedback is just asking for trouble. No one likes being criticized. Feedback is just a recipe for conflict in my opinion, and I have enough of that without looking for it."

Daniel

"Feedback is fine if you feel confident about your judgments. I'm not as competent as some of my staff members in their particular areas of expertise. So do I have a right to say that they're not doing something properly?"

Kelly

"I want to give feedback to one of my staff members about his attitude. I think he's too aggressive. He's in your face all the time. But no one else seems to mind, and it doesn't seem to affect his work."

Ava

"I'd be a fool to give my employees feedback. That's just the sort of excuse they're looking for. If I criticize them, it will just give them license to criticize me, and I'm not going to give them the chance."

But these managers are wrong. Employees can't work effectively without some form of performance feedback.

Effective feedback will:
- enable an objective evaluation of performance,
- encourage workers to improve their performance,
- indicate management concerns to employees,
- make praise meaningful,
- motivate the work force.

Frank and Ernie have had completely different experiences with receiving feedback.

Ernie: I'm new to this division and, after a week, I asked my supervisor to give me some sort of evaluation of how I was doing. He said that he'd have told me if he wasn't satisfied with my performance. Well, I'm still in the dark. I feel a little more confident now, but I can't help worrying.

Frank: My supervisor is great. She regularly tells me how I'm doing, and she always has suggestions for any problems that I have. She works with me every now and then, and every time I can do the job a little bit better. I feel really good about this job!

Question

Ronald hasn't given his staff members much, if any, feedback on their performance. His colleague, Sally, advises him that he's not using a really effective management tool. What are the benefits of giving effective feedback on performance?

Options:

1. Feedback motivates the work force.

2. Feedback enables your staff members to comment on your performance.

3. Feedback gives workers an objective evaluation of their performance.

4. Feedback makes praise meaningful.

5. Feedback encourages improvements in performance.

6. Feedback expresses management concerns to employees.

Answer

In fact, the benefits of feedback are considerable and involve motivation, objective evaluations, meaningful praise, encouragement, and a way to express management concerns.

Option 1: Correct. The employees will be more motivated when they know how they are doing compared to what the company expects of them.

Option 2: Incorrect. Feedback is not about what is being said, it is about what is being received. It is about praising good performance, while identifying areas that need improvement.

Option 3: Correct. Objectivity lends validity to the evaluation of the employees' performance. They will be more likely to make appropriate adjustments.

Option 4: Correct. Meaningful praise strongly motivates people. Employees know that those giving the praise really mean it because it is given in the larger context created by the feedback.

Option 5: Correct. Employees will want to continue receiving positive feedback. Similarly, they will be more likely to want to address areas of improvement that are identified by constructive feedback.

Option 6: Correct. This lends weight to the concerns that are expressed. Employees are more likely to make efforts to change the areas of concern.

Giving feedback effectively has many benefits. Learning how to properly give feedback will help prevent problem performance.

Principles of performance feedback

Principles of performance feedback

Providing feedback is a vital skill for any manager to master. But too often, feedback is poorly used and misunderstood. When this happens, feedback can backfire on the person giving, and the person receiving the feedback.

What do you think about the feedback that Sara is giving Jenny?

Sara: I didn't know you were so inattentive. You must know by now how we do things here. When the procedures state that you can only use the official company logo with permission, that's what it means.

Jenny: But the document I sent wasn't really an official sort of document. I was just doing what the other administrative staff members do.

Sara: Everything is an official document here. I heard that the presentation was also really messy.

Jenny: Do you want to see what I produced? Sara: I don't need to. Don't do it again!

This isn't effective feedback. Sara is just telling Jenny off. She isn't listening and isn't interested in Jenny's explanation. She isn't concerned with Jenny's perception, and she really doesn't have good information.

Effective feedback is giving someone information on the way that he or she acts--both in terms of the results of those actions and the accompanying behavior.

Effective feedback must:
- involve both participants,
- consider different understandings of a situation,
- be nonjudgmental.

If Sara had used these principles to give feedback to Jenny, it would have been very different. See what might have happened.

Sara: I understand that you sent a document without getting permission to use the company logo.

Jenny: Well, it wasn't anything official, and I've seen the other administrative staff members doing the same.

Sara: You need to understand that all documents represent the company, so they must adhere to the highest standards.

Jenny: But everybody does it.

Sara: I can see why you did it, but you must follow the correct procedure. If you have a copy of what you sent, I'd like to look it over with you. I've heard comments about it, but I haven't seen it. So I thought the best thing to do would be to review it together.

This time, when Sara gives Jenny effective feedback, the process involves both of them. This enables Jenny to see a different perspective on her actions, and the feedback is nonjudgmental.

Creating involvement

Involvement is created by dialog. Dialog is best created by using questions, not statements. This sets the right tone for the discussion and enables inaccuracies to be revealed.

Understanding

Effective feedback recognizes that people may interpret situations differently. If managed correctly, feedback can break down insularity and show another side of things.

Being nonjudgmental

Feedback doesn't blame, it investigates. It should start from a nonjudgmental description, and then a dialog should be used to build a judgment of what has happened in the situation. If you start by judging, then dialog is blocked.

Question

Andrew knows that effective feedback must uphold certain principles.

Match each principle to the phrase that characterizes it.

Options:

A. involving participants
B. creating different understandings
C. being nonjudgmental

Targets:

1. investigatory
2. uses questions, not statements
3. breaks down insularity

Answer

Feedback seeks to involve participants by using questions, not statements. Its investigatory nature means it's nonjudgmental, and it can break down insularity by creating new understandings of the same situation.

Being nonjudgmental will help those receiving feedback to not put up their defenses. This will encourage a positive discussion in which people are motivated to make needed improvements.

Involving the participants with questions will help Andrew get the employees thinking about the issues that are brought up. Also, they will be more strongly invested in the conversation.

The different understandings that are created will help to positively shape attitudes and judgments. Those receiving the feedback will be more open to it.

Feedback is an essential skill for any manager. If you stick to the principles outlined, you will give effective feedback that will help to prevent problem performance.

Effective performance feedback techniques

Effective performance feedback techniques

Managers do not have to force effective feedback on employees. Many managers imagine that because feedback is sometimes uncomfortable, their workers do not want or need it. This is entirely wrong. Employees want effective feedback.

Imagine a situation without feedback--for example, golfing in the dark. You don't know where the hole is or whether you hit the golf ball near it. You will quickly lose interest in the task. There is no point to it.

So feedback on performance is something that most employees seek. But it has to be effective feedback, and you must use certain techniques in giving feedback to your employees to ensure that it is effective.

There are three essential characteristics of effective feedback.

Effective identification

For feedback to be effective, the actions and behavior of the worker need to be accurately and clearly identified. Secondhand descriptions do not carry weight. A manager must establish the truth of the behavior by personal and direct observation.

Effective evaluation

Evaluation of performance has to relate to public performance standards that the worker already knows. If you haven't set standards, then you risk being subjective in your evaluation. It's unfair if the worker doesn't know the standards.

Effective development

Effective feedback is not an impasse. You must include a positive outcome to the feedback. Usually, this will mean providing some development opportunities so that performance improves and that employees know they have support to do the best they can.

Maurice, Kelsey, and Diane have received effective feedback from their managers. See how they have benefited from the process.

Maurice: I started to get a bad reputation after one of my close colleagues was dismissed for unsafe work. People assumed that I was guilty of the same offense. So when Charlie said he wanted to spend a day with me, I was really pleased. He could assess my work, not the ignorant opinions about it.

Kelsey: When I started, my managers explained the performance standards in great detail. I know where I stand. I've never had feedback that surprised me. Even when I wasn't performing so well last year, I knew exactly what I had to do. That was a real comfort, and the feedback reinforced my desire to get back on top again.

Problem Performance Management

Diane: The real turning point for me wasn't getting feedback on my performance. I knew I wasn't performing well. It was the support that followed to help me improve that really made the difference. I was given a mentor who went through every one of my processes with me, and together we sorted out the glitches. Now I'm a top performer.

Question

Mitchell is concerned about ensuring that the feedback he gives his staff members is as effective as possible.

What are the characteristics of effective feedback?

Options:

1. Effective feedback must make employees feel uncomfortable.

2. Effective feedback includes a positive outcome.

3. Clear and accurate identification of performance through direct observation is part of effective feedback.

4. Mitchell will have to force feedback on his staff members if it is to be effective.

5. Effective feedback means evaluation of performance against public standards.

Answer

In fact, effective feedback involves identifying and evaluating performance and then offering development opportunities.

Option 1: Incorrect. Mitchell can and should give feedback in a very positive manner that leads to a desire to make improvements.

Option 2: Correct. Having a positive outcome is all about communicating to the employee that they will be supported as they make the needed changes. This will motivate Mitchell's staff towards positive change.

Option 3: Correct. The truth must be identified and simply expressed in a way that lets the employee know it's the truth.

Option 4: Incorrect. Forced feedback will only result in negative results. Mitchell's staff must feel like he wants them to succeed as much as they do, resulting in a very positive interchange.

Option 5: Correct. If the employee is not aware of the standards, feedback cannot be effective. The standards must be the foundation upon which Mitchell delivers his feedback.

To give really effective feedback, like the managers of Maurice, Kelsey, and Diane, you have to not only know what techniques are effective, but also be able to apply them with confidence when you give feedback.

Effective Identification

Be direct, and own your observations by saying, "I saw." Observe more than once. Secondhand comments, by customers for example, are useful in verifying your perceptions. Use specific examples when giving feedback.

Effective Evaluation

Express your evaluation in a neutral tone by comparing it against standards. But try to seek an explanation that puts the performance in context. Evaluation can be daunting, but be confident about performing this essential task.

Effective Development

For feedback to be helpful in improving performance, you should give it as soon as you witness the actions. Describe the issue as a mutual problem, and be positive about developing the means to improve the performance.

Case Study: Question 1 of 3

Problem Performance Management

Scenario

You are a manager at Nutbeems, and you have to give feedback to Sheila on her performance.

She has given you a letter from a customer who has complimented her on her helpfulness, and she has assessed her own performance as excellent in the monthly self-rating review the company has introduced.

Answer these questions, in order, to show how to use effective performance feedback techniques.

Question

Which statements would you use to give effective feedback to Sheila?

Options:

1. "I'm sorry that I haven't spent time with you, but nobody has complained, so I'm sure you're doing really well. Keep up the good work!"

2. "I know that you are keeping all of your customer files up to date. Good work."

3. "Just to be sure my observations are right, I asked another of your customers to comment on your approach. He said that you always suggested possible better alternatives to the product he requested."

4. "Tony Parsons from dispatching says that you don't fill out his forms properly. You'll have to watch that."

5. "I'm going to work with you this week. Then we can discuss any performance issues I've observed."

Answer

In fact, you need to offer specific comments on behavior that you have personally observed. Whenever possible, check out your perceptions with a third party.

Option 1: Incorrect. Comments that are too general, such as this one, come across as insincere. This statement probably won't hold much weight for Sheila.

Option 2: Correct. This statement outlines personal observations that you have made. First-hand witnesses such as this will give weight to what you are about to say to Sheila.

Option 3: Correct. Secondhand comments, by customers for example, are useful in verifying your perceptions.

Option 4: Incorrect. You should not rely on secondhand evidence to make your observations. In order for your feedback to be effective, Sheila must perceive that you have personally verified the information you are presenting.

Option 5: Correct. This will allow you the chance to further observe Sheila's performance. Also, it will communicate to her that you are willing to support her development through any issues that might arise.

Case Study: Question 2 of 3

When you observed Sheila's performance, you noted that she did not always update her records on the CRM database.

How should you use this information to give Sheila feedback?

Options:

1. "Sheila, you didn't complete the CRM database on each customer by the end of the working day, and that's your operating guideline."

2. "Is there a reason why you didn't put all of your information into the CRM database on time?"

Problem Performance Management

3. "Sheila, I'm not an expert on these things, but shouldn't you put more information into the CRM database?"

4. "There's no excuse for the sloppy recording procedures you have got away with in the past. You will complete the records every day before you leave."

Answer

The best techniques for evaluating performance are using a neutral tone, and comparing performance with public and known standards.

Option 1: Correct. By using this statement in a neutral tone, you are describing the issue to Sheila in a direct and concise manner. Also, you are basing your comments on a company standard that is publicly known.

Option 2: Correct. This statement seeks Sheila's understanding of the situation, rather than solely relying on your own. This communicates respect and shows support for Sheila, resulting in higher levels of motivation.

Option 3: Incorrect. Softening your message will communicate a casual attitude on your part. Also, you are not basing your remarks on a known company standard.

Option 4: Incorrect. This statement shows no support for Sheila. It doesn't take her understanding into account and doesn't base the issue on a known company standard.

Case Study: Question 3 of 3

Sheila tells you that she has trouble with some of the coding in the CRM database, which is why she doesn't always fill things in immediately.

How should you reply to her?

Options:

1. "Well, it's a bit late to tell me that now. You attended the same training as everyone else, didn't you?"

2. "The training was quite some time ago, wasn't it? I really should have been more aware of the need to keep refreshing your skills. But you've reminded me, so we can work on it together."

3. "Nobody else thinks it's difficult. You're just not trying hard enough."

4. "I suggest we do the CRM updates together for a while until you understand the coding."

Answer

In fact, you need to look at performance problems as mutual issues that can be improved with a positive approach.

Option 1: Incorrect. This statement has a very negative feeling about it and blames the problem exclusively on Sheila. It would be more effective to use positive terms and look on the problem as an issue that both of you can work on.

Option 2: Correct. This statement was formed in a positive manner and looks at the problem as a mutual problem, rather than resting the blame entirely on Sheila.

Option 3: Incorrect. The negative feeling of this statement is destructive. You would do better to focus on delivering the message in a positive way that looks on the problem as an issue that they can mutually work on.

Option 4: Correct. By offering support to Sheila you are approaching the issue as a mutual challenge. As a result, Sheila will feel more valued, and will respect you more for handling the situation in this manner.

Although Sheila has rated herself highly and her customer agrees, you should ensure that when giving feedback, you base it on your own observations. You should explain to Sheila what you have seen, and get additional feedback from another customer to substantiate your observations.

The fact that Sheila was having difficulty with the database should have given you an opportunity to comment on her performance, but you should have been neutral, and focused on comparing her actions with company standards.

Finally, you should have considered Sheila's problem with resolving her database difficulties as a shared issue. Getting together with her to review the problems and find a resolution was the best way forward.

Don't avoid feedback or assume that the worker is always at fault. Be positive, develop your staff members, and give them real feedback based on company standards. Then you know your feedback will be effective.

Mistakes in giving performance feedback

Mistakes in giving performance feedback

In the Harvard Business Review article, "A Better Way to Deliver Bad News," Jean-Francois Manzoni pointed out that many managers find giving feedback difficult. He also analyzed the common mistakes that they make.

Manzoni argues that the problem for managers stems from the framing of the situation and that this approach subsequently causes other problems. By "framing," Manzoni means the way that managers define the boundaries of the situation that they face.

In terms of feedback, this means the way that a manager considers which issues will be discussed, how the staff member will react, how the problem performance might be solved, and so on.

People usually expect feedback to be difficult and stressful. This means that consciously, or more likely unconsciously, the manager creates a very narrow frame around the feedback. See how Ben gives feedback to Clarrie.

Ben: I've talked to you before about taking on too much work and failing to complete it all. You must delegate more.

Clarrie: But everybody else was too busy trying to complete the Henrickson order!

Ben: I'm not interested in the circumstances this time. I've told you before, you must stop overloading yourself and pass the work on to your team.

Ben's feedback to Clarrie demonstrated narrow framing.

Narrow framing is characterized by:
- the manager's explanation of employee behavior being the only explanation discussed,
- the manager using a binary approach to feedback--there are only two alternatives, win or lose,
- the manager adhering to the original framing, no matter what comes up in the subsequent discussion.

Narrow framing inevitably creates a bad experience in giving and receiving feedback. When faced with this determined and absolute rigidity in the perception of the manager, the employee often fights back, and the conflict between them escalates. When next faced with giving an employee feedback, the manager is even more primed to expect difficulty. To avoid problems, many managers overcompensate and respond with a different, but predictable, set of mistakes.

Easing in

The narrow framing has not disappeared, but the approach is different in that managers now take a "softly softly" approach. They ask a carefully designed set of questions, structured to persuade the employee to provide proof from their own mouth to support the manager's beliefs.

Fundamental attribution error

Managers overemphasize the individual's general personality and character as the cause of the poor performance. They explain the problem performance as a product of these character flaws, and deliberately underestimate other specific conditions that might have caused it.

False consensus effect

Managers assume that all reasonable people will see the problem as they do, and are taken aback when they do not. This shock leads to an escalating difference between the perceptions of the manager and employee. Neither side can value the other's beliefs, so the rift grows.

Ben's experience with Clarrie will affect the next time he gives feedback, even though he meets with Alex this time.

Ben is prompted into making a different set of mistakes. Ben thinks that Alex isn't producing his job advertisements on time.

Ben: Do you think you've got enough time to write the job advertisements?

Alex: Well, it can be time consuming, but I think it's important to get them right.

Ben: I agree. It is really important, but aren't you really busy with the selection interviews?

Alex: Yes, but I can fit it all in.

Problem Performance Management

Ben: Well, you're a bit behind with them. I know you're a perfectionist, but you must produce the job advertisements a lot quicker.

Alex: No, that's not it at all. I've had real difficulty getting the job details from finance. That's why I've been behind with the advertisements.

Ben: You have to stop trying to make each one a work of art. Getting the basic information in the ad is good enough.

Ben tried to get Alex to agree with his belief that the problem was due to Alex's attention to detail, and couldn't believe that Alex did not see things the way he did. By trying to compensate for the mistakes he made in giving feedback to Clarrie, Ben developed another set of problems.

What could Ben and other managers like him do to avoid all of these common mistakes?

Narrow Framing

Diminish narrow framing by challenging your own preconceptions. Listen to your employees' views and opinions. Accept that employees may respond differently from your expectations, and vary your responses accordingly.

Easing In

Easing in means using questions to elicit specific answers. This backfires when the answers you get aren't the ones you want. If you respond genuinely to the answers that are given, whether they are in the form you expect or not, you will avoid easing in.

Fundamental Attribution Error

To avoid false attribution error, you must downplay the assumption that personality and character are the main causes of problem performance. You need to accept that the context in which the performance occurs can have a significant effect on it.

False Consensus Effect

To avoid false consensus, you must acknowledge that a subordinate's perception of the situation can vary from your own. This does not mean that you cannot disagree, but you must try to build bridges and support your employee in spite of your differences.

Question

Terry has just experienced some difficult feedback interviews with members of his team. When he reflects on the problems with the feedback, he can see that he has made some common mistakes. Match each type of mistake to its corresponding characteristic.

Options:

A. narrow framing
B. easing in
C. fundamental attribution error
D. false consensus effect

Targets:

1. Managers take a "softly softly" approach.
2. The explanations do not differ from the one held by the manager.
3. There is an assumption that all reasonable people will agree on the issue.
4. Managers overemphasize the significance of personality.

Answer

In narrow framing, the manager only considers one interpretation, and false consensus relies on the idea of "all reasonable people." Fundamental attribution error relates to personality, and easing in involves the "softly softly" approach.

Easing in is asking a set of questions to which the only right answer is the one the manager wants. To avoid this, Terry should respond genuinely to the answers given by the employees.

Terry can overcome narrow framing by challenging his own preconceptions on the issue. Also, he can listen more closely to the employees opinions. He might find out that their thoughts on the matter are not the same as his.

False consensus effect refers to making the mistake of presuming that there is agreement on an issue. It is possible that a subordinate is in disagreement. This situation calls for giving support and withholding criticism.

Terry can avoid placing the blame on the employees' personalities by recognizing that there is a larger context that is likely affecting them. This context could change the way he looks at the problem.

Case Study: Question 1 of 3
Scenario

You are going to give feedback to Leonora about the untidiness of her desk. You are concerned because important files are stacked everywhere. Leonora also has a reputation for being lazy, and you think this is why her desk is so untidy.

You will then give some feedback to Francis.

Answer these questions, in order, to show how you're going to avoid mistakes in giving them feedback on their performance.

Question

What approaches would you take to giving Leonora feedback?

Options:

1. I know that she gets easily upset when challenged, so I will take a soft approach to confronting her laziness.

2. Leonora has a reputation for being lazy, but I am going to deliberately put that aside and discuss the security aspects of leaving files everywhere.

3. I am going to ask her whether she has any problems with keeping her desk tidier.

4. Leonora is lazy, so I'll have to threaten her about cleaning her desk, or she won't do it.

5. I'm going to be flexible in my approach to giving her feedback, and see how she responds to my suggestions.

Answer

In fact, you need to diminish narrow framing on your behalf by refusing to follow preconceptions about Leonora, and asking for, and responding to, her perceptions about the problem.

Option 1: Incorrect. This is an example of easing in to the feedback. Easing in can be avoided by giving a genuine response to the employee's answers, even if they are different than the answers you expected.

Option 2: Correct. By putting aside any preconceived notions you avoid narrowly framing the problem.

Option 3: Correct. Feedback is more constructive when you seek to find out the employee's perceptions of the problem.

Option 4: Incorrect. This feedback will not be effective. It is better to elicit responses from the employee and determine what they think the problem is. Be flexible and supportive in determining a solution.

Option 5: Correct. Approaching the feedback session with an open mind and a willingness to sincerely consider the employee's responses will ensure a positive experience for you and the employee.

Case Study: Question 2 of 3

You have had some bad experiences with giving feedback due to narrow framing on your behalf. Now you have to give feedback to Francis. You are concerned that his telephone manner seems abrupt, even though he says that he's just providing factual answers to customers. Which statements would be appropriate to use in giving feedback to him?

Options:

1. "So what do you think your customers think of you?"

2. "Are your calls to customers in response to complaints they have made about products? Are they angry before you have even spoken to them?"

3. "Aren't customers put off by your abrupt attitude?"

4. "I agree that angry customers need factual answers, but it could sound abrupt."

Answer

You need to emphasize the context of Francis' problem, not his personality, to avoid a fundamental attribution error. You also need to respond to his answer, and not ease in by avoiding the real issue.

Option 1: Incorrect. This question is an example of easing in. It is designed to elicit a specific response. It is better to ask questions that lead to thoughtful answers from the employee and then respond genuinely to those answers.

Option 2: Correct. This question will prompt Francis to reflect upon the situation and then give genuine answers.

You can acknowledge his answers and the feedback session will be a positive and productive experience.

Option 3: Incorrect. This question shows that the feedback session has been approached with an attitude that is narrowly framed. This could lead to easing in and a fundamental attribution error.

Option 4: Correct. This answer indicates that the employee's perspective has been considered and is being genuinely responded to. It is a productive way to give feedback.

Case Study: Question 3 of 3

When you tell Francis that customers want factual information, he responds by saying that he is also as succinct as possible.

Which responses would be appropriate to use in giving feedback to him now?

Options:

1. "I think it's really important to engage the customer in a conversation. Everybody knows that's a fundamental quality of customer service. I can't believe you don't see it!"

2. "I don't agree that the best way to deal with an angry customer is to be as succinct as possible."

3. "No, there's no room for discussion here. I insist that you try to engage the customer in more conversation."

4. "I think we can find common ground on the need for a factual approach, and discuss ways for you to be more conversational."

Answer

In fact, you have to show that you are not seeking false consensus by being prepared to disagree with Francis.

Problem Performance Management

You also need to remember that it is possible to disagree and build bridges between your respective positions.

Option 1: Incorrect. It is more productive to respond to the employee's viewpoint. This answer does not include any of Francis' perspective.

Option 2: Correct. This is a perfect opportunity to avoid a false consensus. It is acceptable to disagree with the employee on this point and then to construct a positive working relationship and support your employee in spite of the disagreement.

Option 3: Incorrect. Feedback that is not sensitive to the views of the employee will backfire.

Option 4: Correct. This is a great example of a way to include an employee's concerns and viewpoint and then support them in making the changes that are needed.

It would have been easy to frame your feedback to Leonora narrowly, on the basis of your preconceptions about her laziness. Instead, you should have asked for her views and listened to her feelings about the issue. And when it came to dealing with Francis, you should have been direct to avoid easing in, and ensured that you looked at the context of the issue by asking questions about the customer complaints. You also should have accepted that Francis' view might be different from yours, and you should have disagreed amicably.

It's easy to approach feedback from a narrow frame and then to subsequently compound this as a result of negative experiences of feedback. Apply the skills taught in this lesson, and you will avoid these mistakes.

CHAPTER 2 - Problem Performance Identification

CHAPTER 2 - Problem Performance Identification

Section 1 - Performance Issues
Section 2 - Causes of Problem Performance
Section 3 - Measuring Performance

Section 1 - Performance Issues

Performance management is not a neutral subject. It is fraught with arguments about the best way to turn underperforming employees into exceptional workers.

It's important for managers to distinguish between conduct and performance. The distinction characterizes a debate about the most effective way to treat problem performance. Should the response to problem performance be punishment, or should managers attempt to help and support workers to perform better?

Is there a way to identify poor performers based on their personalities? In fact, most of the research on performance tends to concentrate on good performers.

Although the conclusions aren't foolproof, some research results suggest that personality traits of poor performers are, in part, the opposite of personality traits of good performers.

The idea of forced ranking systems is one of the most debated issues in performance management.

The forced ranking system identifies employee performance through a conventional appraisal system, but then the employees' scores are distributed into a bell curve, or normal distribution curve, with fixed bands--a top band, a middle band, and so on.

Controversial issues

Controversial issues

Performance management is not a neutral subject. It is fraught with arguments about the best way to turn underperforming employees into exceptional workers.

Roy and Angela are two managers at MJK Inc. They both have problem performers on their teams. Follow their conversation.

Roy: I should have known. I hired someone who was obviously very quiet and reserved. I know that if you want high level performers, you have to hire extroverts.

Angela: Oh, come on. You don't honestly believe that our noisy staff members are better workers than our quiet ones?

Roy: I think personality has a lot to do with performance.

Angela: That's just crazy talk! I want to base my actions on something more concrete. Promote the workers at the top, and punish the workers at the bottom. That's what works!

Roy: No way! You can't manage by fear. You've got to help people improve. You can't punish them into becoming brilliant workers.

The argument between Roy and Angela shows that the issues surrounding problem performance at work can cause controversies.

- Should problem performance be improved by punishing, or by helping?
- Can you identify problem performers based on personality?
- Are forced ranking systems ethical? Are they useful?

These questions, and the arguments that surround them, are important to an organization deciding on its approach to performance management, and the way that it manages its largest resource: the workforce.

This lesson is designed to help you refine your views about performance problems by exploring the controversial issues surrounding them.

By addressing these controversial issues related to performance, you will:

- be up to date with the latest views about performance management practices,
- avoid some of the common mistakes in performance management,
- be able to design a performance management system that incorporates good practice.

Question

Naomi feels that performance management is too contentious an area to discuss with her colleagues. What

Problem Performance Management

are the benefits of Naomi addressing the major controversial issues related to problem performance?

Options:

1. She will avoid some of the common mistakes in performance management.
2. She will make people notice her by addressing the contentious issues related to performance management.
3. She will be up to date with the latest practices in performance management.
4. She will be able to design a performance management system that adheres to good practice.
5. She will avoid arguments with co-workers about performance management.

Answer

In fact, the benefits for Naomi of addressing the controversies related to performance management are keeping up to date, avoiding mistakes, and incorporating good practice into her systems.

Option 1: Correct. If Naomi doesn't address these issues, she will likely repeat the mistakes other managers have made in performance management. Taking a preventative approach will help her avoid common pitfalls.

Option 2: Incorrect. Performance management is about helping the employees to better their performance, not about Naomi drawing attention to herself.

Option 3: Correct. Naomi will learn of others' success stories and useful techniques, which she can then apply to her own organization.

Option 4: Correct. Addressing major controversies first will give Naomi insights that will help her design a better system to manage employees' performance.

Option 5: Incorrect. Addressing the major controversial issues up front will not discourage employees from arguing with Naomi about her performance management techniques.

You may have a natural tendency to shy away from controversial topics at work. But don't avoid this one! Explore the contentious issues related to identifying problem performance at work, and you will discover real benefits.

Conduct problems and performance problems

Conduct problems and performance problems

It's important for managers to distinguish between conduct and performance. The distinction characterizes a debate about the most effective way to treat problem performance.

Should the response to problem performance be punishment, or should managers attempt to help and support workers to perform better?

What is the difference between conduct and performance?

Conduct

A problem with conduct involves the violation of organization rules.

Performance

A problem with performance involves a failure to do the job at an acceptable level.

All organizations have rules and standards of acceptable behavior. For example, one of the most common rules in organizations relates to attendance. When staff members are late, they are not performing badly--they are just breaking a rule. Examples of conduct problems include:
- insubordination
- excessive absenteeism
- theft
- fighting.

Performance includes issues such as the quality and quantity of work. For example, workers have performance problems when they do not complete expected work in a given period of time. Other performance problems might include producing substandard work, provoking customer complaints, or wasting an organization's resources.

The definitions show that each of these categories of problems can be independent of each other. A worker who is late may perform well on the job, so a conduct problem does not automatically present a performance problem. Similarly, a performance problem may be encountered in someone who never has any conduct problems. But what is the value of this distinction for the manager? The value lies in determining the approach to handling the problem.

Approaches to conduct problems

A conduct problem is one that is more likely to result in an immediate sanction, even one at a low level. The assumption is that a worker has willfully broken the rules of the organization, which requires some corresponding punishment.

Approaches to performance problems

Problem Performance Management

A performance problem does not automatically require some form of sanction because it usually is not willful. The response includes seeking ways to support the individual through counseling, coaching, and training toward better performance.

Angela and Roy are discussing the performance problems of some of their staff members.

Roy: Sue's been late twice this week. I wonder if I should send her to a time management training course?

Angela: You're kidding. She's late; it's against company policy, and that's it. She needs a warning about her conduct.

Roy: Yeah, but what about the way you treated Robert? You sent him to a time management course.

Angela: I know, but that was different. He couldn't prioritize his work. He used to come in early and stay late, but he still couldn't get everything done on time. He was struggling to do the best he could, and we needed to help him.

Roy: Well, you couldn't say that about Sue. I think she just cuts her commuting time too short. She just needs to leave a few minutes earlier.

Angela: There's a big difference between Sue and Robert's problems, and we shouldn't confuse them.

Question

Stella and Karl can't agree on their response to a staff member who refuses to use the company safety equipment. Stella says that it's a conduct problem. Karl says it's a performance problem. Help them by matching each type of problem performance to one or more of its corresponding characteristics.

Options:

A. conduct problem
B. performance problem

Targets:

1. a violation of company rules
2. failure to do the job at an acceptable level
3. usually not willful
4. respond with sanctions
5. support improvement by training

Answer

Actually, performance problems are concerned with quality and quantity of work, and conduct problems are the result of breaking rules. You should respond to them differently.

If Stella and Karl's company has a rule requiring the use of safety equipment, and the staff member willfully chooses to disobey that rule, his conduct is not appropriate and should be addressed.

Performance problems are about productivity. If the staff member is not meeting production standards, the problem won't normally be addressed through warnings or other sanctions.

Performance problems are due to the employee's inability to perform job tasks sufficiently. This often comes from factors beyond the employee's control.

A violation of company rules is a conduct problem that will likely result in some sort of sanction directed toward the staff member.

Employees who exhibit performance problems probably need some company-sponsored training to become fully productive. This intervention should be considered support, not punishment.

Problem Performance Management

It is vital that you distinguish between conduct and performance problems. Otherwise, your response to them will be wrong, and you may exacerbate the problem.

Personality traits linked to performance

Personality traits linked to performance

Is there a way to identify poor performers based on their personalities?

In fact, most of the research on performance tends to concentrate on good performers.

Although the conclusions aren't foolproof, some research results suggest that personality traits of poor performers are, in part, the opposite of personality traits of good performers.

Question

Tony remembers the acronym, OCEAN, for the five major personality factors, but he can't associate forms of behavior with each of the factors. Help him by matching each personality factor with its corresponding behavior.

Options:

A. openness to experience
B. conscientiousness

C. extroversion
D. agreeableness
E. neuroticism

Targets:
1. dependable
2. cooperative
3. creative
4. anxious
5. assertive

Answer

Conscientiousness refers to how people complete their work. Conscientious people pay attention to detail, maintain high levels of accuracy, and can be counted on to finish. They are also hard workers.

Being cooperative is one of the characteristics of an agreeable person. An agreeable person is also amiable and pleasant to be with.

People who are open to experience are generally creative, curious, and cultured. They also tend to be imaginative in their work.

People who are rated high on neuroticism tend to be anxious, nervous, depressed, and emotional.

Extroversion defines people who characteristically are outgoing, like to be around people, and are assertive.

In the past, the most common predictor of performance was considered to be intelligence. There is still significant truth to this idea, but other facets of personality as predictors of performance have gained credibility in the past few years. In part, this is a product of an agreement among psychologists about the personality factors that are consistently present, and important, in the human personality across national and cultural boundaries.

Openness to experience
Openness to experience defines individuals who are creative, curious, and cultured as opposed to individuals with an unimaginative orientation, and relatively narrow interests.

Conscientiousness
Conscientiousness measures the extent to which individuals are hardworking, organized, dependable, and persevering as opposed to lazy, disorganized, and unreliable.

Extroversion
Extroversion concerns the extent to which individuals are gregarious, sociable, assertive, and active as opposed to reserved, timid, and quiet.

Agreeableness
Agreeableness concerns the degree to which individuals are cooperative, warm, and agreeable as opposed to cold, disagreeable, and antagonistic.

Neuroticism
Neuroticism concerns the degree to which the individual is insecure, anxious, depressed, and emotional as opposed to calm, self-confident, and cool.

The employees who work on the IT help desk team at Delstone Casings exhibit the five most significant personality factors.

Openness to experience
Oliver is a really cautious worker. He follows the guidelines to the letter. He never deviates from the instructions on his screen, and relays them in exactly the prescribed order. Oliver is rated low on openness to experience.

Extroversion

Miranda is really shy. She doesn't engage in much conversation with callers. She sticks to the business at hand, and gets embarrassed if anyone tries to draw her out. Miranda is rated low on extroversion.

Conscientiousness

Claire has a reputation for persevering with customer problems, and seeing them through to the end. She gives her instructions carefully, and always makes sure the caller understands before she moves on. Claire is rated high on conscientiousness.

Agreeableness

Andy is very polite. He is concerned when software causes problems. He researches problems on his own time to support the callers, but he hates to take any credit. Andy is rated high on agreeableness.

Neuroticism

Nora is the cool and laid-back member of the team. She is confident in her ability to handle problems, and always seems to be able to calm down the agitated callers. Nora is rated low on neuroticism.

Using these factors, researchers identified small correlations between some personality traits and workplace performance. Success in performance training also was a factor linked to personality. In some cases, the correlation between personality and performance applied across all occupational groups, but in others, the correlation applied only to certain jobs.

Openness to experience

Openness to experience is a valid predictor of good performance for police and skilled-labor jobs. It also is a valid predictor of training success.

Conscientiousness

Conscientiousness is a predictor of good performance for all occupational groups except for creative occupations, such as artist or musician. Then this factor can be detrimental to performance.

Extroversion

Extroversion predicts positive performance for managers and police.

Agreeableness

Agreeableness shows the lowest relationship to employee success, with a correlation of almost zero. But it is associated with training success.

Emotional stability

Emotional stability, the positive behavior of the neuroticism factor, is a predictor of good performance across all occupational groups.

So the most significant correlation involves conscientiousness and emotional stability as indicators of positive performance at work.

Angela and Roy are discussing the personality traits they consider to be most likely to lead to good performance at work.

Angela: I look for intelligence first and foremost.

Roy: Yes, that's sensible. But I think that besides intelligence, I'd also

Angela: You mean you just want someone who's going to be a painstaking plodder? That wouldn't work for me. I want bright, enthusiastic, and lively people.

Roy: Well, maybe that's because we're recruiting for different jobs. You're recruiting creative people, whereas I'm looking for administrators.

Angela: That makes sense. But I also want staff members who are calm and relaxed. The creative temperament can be a bit neurotic sometimes!

Roy: I agree. "Calm and conscientious" would describe my ideal employee.

Don't forget that the correlations being described are small. This link between personality and performance comes with no guarantees. Other factors, such as training, resources, and relationships, can easily affect performance in spite of personality. Moreover, the identification of these personality traits is complex and demanding, and requires the use of psychometric tests with psychological interpretation.

Question

Suzie wants to take a more scientific approach to recruitment, using tests to assess the personalities of candidates to predict their performance.

She says research suggests links between some personality factors and performance. Which statements correctly identify those links?

Options:

1. Extroversion predicts the performance of scientists.

2. Conscientiousness is predictive of employee performance over most occupational groups.

3. Openness to experience is not a valid predictor of training success.

4. Agreeableness shows the lowest relationship to employee success.

5. Emotional stability is a positive predictor of performance across all occupational groups.

Answer

In fact, emotional stability and conscientiousness are the most valid predictors of performance, and agreeableness does not predict performance.

Option 1: Incorrect. Extroversion predicts positive performance for managers and police officers. Option 2: Correct. Most jobs are done better by hard-working employees who complete their work and pay attention to detail.

Option 3: Incorrect. Openness to experience is a good predictor of training success because of the need to learn new things.

Option 4: Correct. The relationship between employee success and agreeableness is almost zero. Agreeableness does predict good training success, however.

Option 5: Correct. Emotional stability refers to a lack of neurosis. It has the best correlation with employee performance.

Personality does seem to be related to performance. For many people, the idea that a conscientious and emotionally stable personality would make an effective worker seems obvious.

But the support of scientific research adds validity to the claim. The personalities of prospective employees can be used as a way to predict their performance.

Forced ranking systems

Forced ranking systems

The idea of forced ranking systems is one of the most debated issues in performance management.

The forced ranking system identifies employee performance through a conventional appraisal system, but then the employees' scores are distributed into a bell curve, or normal distribution curve, with fixed bands--a top band, a middle band, and so on.

An example of employee distribution within these bands might be 10 percent in the top band, 15 percent in the next band, 50 percent in the middle band, 15 percent in the band just below, and 10 percent in the bottom band.

After worker performance has been evaluated, the goal of the process is to get rid of employees in the bottom band, reward the high achievers, and repeat this process every year.

Question

Which statement is an accurate description of the forced ranking process?

Options:

1. The forced ranking system requires managers to rate their employees on aptitude.

2. The forced ranking system requires managers to rate their employees, and then distribute their scores into fixed bands.

3. The forced ranking system requires managers to distribute their comments to all employees.

4. The forced ranking system requires managers to choose who should lead each team.

Answer

In fact, a forced ranking system requires managers to distribute the assessments of their employees into fixed bands.

Option 1: Incorrect. The forced ranking system uses a bell curve to rank employees after they have been evaluated using a conventional rating system.

Option 2: Correct. Using conventional methods, managers rate their employees and then distribute the scores over a bell curve. This results in employees being grouped into bands.

Option 3: Incorrect. A forced ranking system deals with employee performance, not with communication between managers and employees.

Option 4: Incorrect. The forced ranking system is not used to develop leadership. It is designed to rate employee performance.

Jack Welch, former CEO of General Electric, is a strong advocate of the forced ranking system. Edward E.

Lawler III, major contributor to theory, research, and practice in the fields of human resources management, is a critic.

Jack Welch

Jack Welch said, "...leaders must...encourage, inspire, and reward that top 20 percent...they must develop the determination to change out...that bottom 10 percent..."

Edward E Lawler III

Edward E. Lawler III said, "Systems that force managers to cut a certain percentage of their people often don't reveal the root causes of problems...and can ultimately be counterproductive."

Arguments for the forced ranking system are based on the excellent performers in the organization, the impact the system has on managers, and the organization as a whole.

Excellent performers

Forced ranking systems are based not only on removing poor performers but also on rewarding excellent ones. Recognition and reward are essential to motivating and retaining high flyers.

Managers

A forced ranking system makes managers do their jobs properly, and appraise effectively. They have to make tough, but necessary, judgments about the performance of their workers that they might otherwise avoid.

The organization

Forced ranking is a competitive and progressive system. By applying it, productivity is improved year after year. Poor performance will not be tolerated as it is in so many companies, and efficiency and effectiveness will increase.

There also are some powerful arguments against the forced ranking approach. They are based on the technical limitations of the approach, and on the weakness of some managers in implementing the system.

Inappropriate use of the bell curve

Forced ranking may fail to work for the department that has an unusual number of outstanding employees, because managers must choose a particular number of employees to rank at the bottom of the scale, regardless of whether they achieve high levels of performance.

Legality

The approach is legally contentious. Some think that forced rankings discriminate against some groups because the impact of such a system falls disproportionately on them. Class actions have been taken against Ford Motor Company, resulting in a settlement of $10.5 million.

Progressive problems

Over time, companies should theoretically reach a point at which managers have weeded out their poor performers, but would still be forced to place good performers in the bottom percentage.

Managerial implementation

Managers may disown their part in the appraisal system. They argue that, although they know an individual is not really a bad performer, they had to pick someone to go into the lower bands. Other managers may retain poor performers so they can fire them at forced ranking time.

Managers and workers have different beliefs about, and attitudes toward, forced ranking systems in their organizations. Martin is a top-performing employee, and Dee is a newly appointed manager. They support the forced ranking system. April is the human resources director for a multinational firm, and Bill is a manager in an organization using the system. They are against forced rankings.

Martin

"I just read a survey that said 32 percent of employees felt that poor performance is tolerated in their companies. Well, that's not true here! We don't tolerate bad performance. Why should we? We remove the worst year after year. So only the best are left."

Dee

"I have to say that in my last organization, appraisals were a joke. No one paid much attention to them. Here, they really matter. I have to back up my evaluations with rewards and dismissals. That certainly focuses everybody's attention."

April

"There's no way we are going to use forced rankings. Look at Conoco and Microsoft. Microsoft settled because its system was considered to be discriminatory on grounds of race; Conoco was said to favor foreign workers over U.S. nationals. It's a dangerous area."

Bill

"It just doesn't make sense. When we first started using forced rankings, I think it really helped weed out the poor performers. Now they're gone, but I still have to assign some people, who are performing perfectly well, to the poor category."

Question

Leonie isn't sure about the use of forced ranking in her organization. She knows there are arguments for and against its use. Help Leonie by matching the arguments to one or more of the examples.

Options:

A. argument for forced ranking

B. argument against forced ranking

Targets:

1. Managers keep bad performers to fire at forced ranking time.

2. Recognition and reward are essential to motivate and retain good performers.

3. Rankings discriminate against some groups.

4. Over time, companies will weed out their poor performers.

5. Efficiency and effectiveness will increase year after year.

Answer

To avoid having to fire good performers, managers will maintain their poor performers so they have someone they can fire at forced ranking time.

An employee who is performing well needs to receive positive reinforcement. The forced ranking system is one way of achieving this.

Because certain groups of people consistently fall into the bottom band of the ranking, firing the people in that bottom band discriminates against those groups.

One of the advantages of using a forced ranking system is that Leonie's organization eliminates the bottom band, which is 10% of the workforce. Doing this each year weeds out the poor performers.

Because the forced ranking system eliminates inefficient workers and rewards the best performers, efficiency and effectiveness increase each year.

Problem Performance Management

Forced ranking systems are subject to a great deal of debate. You now have the tools to carefully consider the advantages and disadvantages of applying such a system in your organization.

Section 2 - Causes of Problem Performance

Imagine this situation: One of your team members is a problem performer. You ask her, "If your life depended on it, could you perform better?" The answer reflects the causes of problem performance, and is also a good indication of the value of knowing the causes of performance problems.

The cause of problem performance for an employee who could improve if her life depended on it is quite different from the cause of problem performance for an employee who can't improve, whatever the price!

When faced with performance problems at work, it's common to blame individual worker error or incompetence. But some problems are in a different category. These problems are due to the working environment--the system.

According to the Merriam-Webster Dictionary, aptitude is "the natural ability" to perform a task. Aptitude problems stem from a problem with a worker's ability or a problem in the task.

Can you sing? Well, many people can sing, but can you become an opera singer? Opera singing requires more than a good voice. It requires you to sing in large halls, often in a different language, and as part of a dramatic presentation. To be an effective opera singer, you need the ability to sing as the operatic task demands.

How often have you heard that a worker who is not performing well has an attitude problem? It's one of the most common descriptions, and explanations, for problem performance at work. But using the brief description "attitude problem" may not be very useful.

You need to differentiate between the types of attitude problems if you are going to improve performance.

When people are accused of having attitude problems, it generally means that they can do the job, but are choosing not to. They have the relevant ability, and system problems are not the cause of problem performance, but they are still not performing adequately.

The causes of problem performance at work

The causes of problem performance at work

Imagine this situation: One of your team members is a problem performer. You ask her, "If your life depended on it, could you perform better?" The answer reflects the causes of problem performance, and is also a good indication of the value of knowing the causes of performance problems.

The cause of problem performance for an employee who could improve if her life depended on it is quite different from the cause of problem performance for an employee who can't improve, whatever the price!

There are three main causes of problem performance:
- system causes, which are not the worker's fault,
- aptitude causes, some of which can be improved by training,
- attitude causes, in which an employee chooses not to perform well.

Problem Performance Management

The way you tackle the problem, and the effectiveness of your approach are both dependent on correctly identifying problem performance. If you get it wrong, you are wasting training on a worker who does not care!

Meryl correctly identified the causes of problem performance in her team members, but Sheila didn't. Review their conversation.

Meryl: I thought Derek was just lazy, at least compared with the other team members. But then I found out that his computer had a recurring glitch, and the help desk staff had given up. He had to reboot every hour. No wonder he was slower than the rest of the team members.

Sheila: You think you've got problems? I've got Ed on my team. I sent him to a refresher course to update his product knowledge. Well, he didn't attend a number of the classes because he got the times wrong. Now I have to send him to another course.

Meryl: Are you sure he's worth it? It sounds to me like he's got an attitude problem. Sending him to any number of courses won't improve his performance if he has an attitude problem.

Question

Meryl tries to explain to Sheila the benefits of identifying the causes of problem performance at work. Which points should Meryl make to convince Sheila?

Options:

1. You spend less time on aptitude problems because there's nothing you can do about them.

2. It prevents you from blaming the workers when the cause is a system problem, and not their fault.

3. You concentrate on the workers with bad attitudes who blame it all on the system.

4. You can distinguish the workers who cannot perform well from those who choose not to.

5. You don't waste time on the issues you can't fix.

Answer

In fact, by identifying the causes of performance problems, you can stop inappropriate blame, determine the workers with attitude problems, and focus on the problems that you can fix.

Option 1: Incorrect. It is important to determine if performance problems are related to aptitude, but there is something you can do about them. Aptitude problems may be helped by training.

Option 2: Correct. Sometimes poor performance is a result of a problem in the system, which employees have no control over.

Option 3: This is not a point that Meryl should make. Identifying the cause of performance problems will help Sheila determine if some of the problems are caused by bad attitudes, not encourage her to concentrate on workers with bad attitudes.

Option 4: Correct. It is a great advantage to be able to identify workers who are likely to improve their performance if they receive help and support.

Option 5: Correct. Identifying the cause of problem performance helps managers to focus their time and energy effectively.

Identifying the causes of problem performance will save you significant time, and more effectively focus your efforts.

Systemic causes of problem performance

Systemic causes of problem performance

When faced with performance problems at work, it's common to blame individual worker error or incompetence. But some problems are in a different category. These problems are due to the working environment--the system.

There are three main causes of system performance problems.

Lack of data

Data refers to the information workers need to perform their jobs, including detailed expectations about their performance. This usually comes in the form of procedures, standards, and timelines. Feedback is also vital data, and must be frequent, detailed, accurate, and timely.

Inadequate tools and resources

Workers need certain tools and resources to do their jobs. Tools include the obvious, such as specific equipment needed to perform a task. Resources must include enough time to perform the task, and the timely availability of quality supplies and raw materials.

Inefficient procedures

Inefficient procedures refer to the flow of work among colleagues, which may have an effect on the final product. In addition, policies and procedures implemented by the organization may affect performance; for example, procedures related to worker health and safety.

These causes of performance problems are common in many organizations.

Lack of data

Ernie knew that he had performance problems caused by the system when the equipment inventories sent to him by each site didn't list radios. The site supervisors didn't know that they were responsible for all communication equipment.

Inadequate tools and resources

The interviews for surveyors were chaotic. Marie realized that it was caused by the system when she discovered that the clerk also had to administer four training courses on the day she was supposed to be hosting the interviews.

Inefficient procedures

The policy for new drivers required them to complete three trips with a senior driver before going solo. This policy was rigorously applied, so even recently retired drivers who were rehired had to undergo the trips with the senior driver.

Problem Performance Management

Ineffectively communicated expectations caused a performance problem for Ernie. His staff just didn't have the data to perform properly. Marie's team was handicapped by the lack of time it was allocated to administer the interviews. It was a system fault because the resources were inadequate.

And the policy regarding new drivers was counterproductive when it meant that experienced drivers had to waste time on three unnecessary training drives.

Question

Jonathan doesn't want anyone to blame his staff members for problem performance caused by the system in his organization. So he has made sure he can clearly identify the causes of difficulties that stem from the system.

Which statements characterize system causes of problem performance?

Options:

1. The team doesn't have the resources or equipment that the company should have provided.

2. Policies and procedures impinge on performance.

3. The company is too systematic in its use of performance appraisals.

4. Staff members don't have the information they need to perform properly.

5. Staff members are not blamed for performance problems.

Answer

In fact, the system causes of problem performance are lack of data, inadequate resources, and inefficient procedures.

Option 1: Correct. One of the three main causes of system performance problems is the lack of tools or resources.

Option 2: Correct. Company procedures, like the way work flows between employees, and company policies, like health and safety procedures, can create system problems that cause poor performance.

Option 3: Incorrect. Performance appraisals refer to the individual performance of each employee. A system cause of problem performance is one that is caused by the work environment, not the individual.

Option 4: Correct. Staff members need information in the form of expectations and feedback, so they can meet the organization's job standards.

Option 5: Incorrect. A system cause of problem performance results from the way the company is functioning. It has nothing to do with the performance of individual staff members.

To recognize performance problems caused by the system, you need to recognize their symptoms.

Lack of data

Note performance levels that are completely unexpected, whether they are good or bad. Also look for performance that adheres to a different standard. And if workers are actively seeking feedback, then the system is probably not providing it.

Inadequate tools and resources

The most obvious sign of this cause is workers who simply can't perform at all. But of equal significance is performance which is hard to predict, alternately high and low, which indicates that the supply chain is not organized and consistent.

Problem Performance Management

Inefficient procedures

When policies and procedures impinge on performance, the clearest sign is that production takes far longer than expected. This is often accompanied by unexpected cost overruns.

Ernie and Marie from Construction King Inc. are telling Richie, a colleague, how to recognize the system causes of problem performance.

Ernie: I'm worried about the way my supervisors have been reacting to any illness on their teams. They visit each person who calls in sick at home. That's too much. I don't expect them to do that--our policy states that we only visit people with recurring absences from illness.

Richie: But surely you want to eliminate unnecessary absences, and this will do it. Are you telling me that because the supervisors are really paying attention to detail, you think there might be a performance problem?

Marie: Ernie's supervisors are demonstrating that they don't know the standard that they are supposed to meet. Sometimes you need to look into a situation further. When I started receiving a wide range of evaluations for one particular trainer, I knew I needed to investigate. One day he received great evaluations; the next day he received poor ones.

Richie: Well, surely that was his fault!

Marie: No. I found out that he had been moved to a different room. He got good reports in the first room, and poor in the second. It didn't take rocket science to figure out that the second room was too crowded. It didn't have the proper equipment, and the trainees hated it.

Ernie: That's true. You have to look deeper sometimes to discover the real causes of poor performance. When I noticed that the costs for uniforms had increased significantly, I found out that our buyer had to use a particular supplier because it was the only one on the new approved supplier list.

Richie: So?

Ernie: The buyer overspent on his budget through no fault of his own. Someone in finance changed the procedures, and the buyer had to use the most expensive supplier. The problem was caused by the system, not him.

Ernie and Marie showed Richie how to look beyond the simple explanations for problem performance, and recognize symptoms of system causes for production failures. They noted that unexpected behavior is often a sign, because with effectively communicated performance standards, there should be no surprises. They picked up on irregular performance as a possible indicator of inadequate resources, and pointed out that procedures can have a serious effect on performance.

Case Study: Question 1 of 3

Scenario

You have been asked to examine performance problems at the warehouses of The Durban Company. Customers have complained about goods consistently arriving late. In some cases, goods were packed so badly that they were broken in transit. You interview Terri, the warehouse manager, to establish what is happening.

Answer the questions to analyze the causes of the problem performance.

Question

Terri tells you she isn't sure what's wrong. She says her workers are conscientious. They're always asking for feedback, and she is constantly surprised by the results

Problem Performance Management

they produce. For example, they implemented a system for using recyclable materials in packaging, creating some imaginative solutions. What responses would you give to Terri?

Options:

1. "When workers ask for feedback, that shows they want to perform well. So if there is no problem with their attitudes, their performance will probably improve."

2. "I'm concerned that your workers have to ask for feedback. That means that existing feedback isn't effective, and they're not getting the data they need to perform well."

3. "I'd worry if you weren't getting exceptional results sometimes. We needn't concern ourselves with exceptional results, even if you didn't expect them."

4. "If you're getting exceptional results that surprise you, then something is wrong with the workers' perceptions of performance standards."

Answer

In fact, you should have noted two symptoms that show the effect on performance of a lack of data. These workers are asking for more feedback, and producing unexpected, exceptional results.

Option 1: Incorrect. The request for feedback is a symptom suggesting that employees need better feedback.

Option 2: Correct. The request for feedback is a symptom of a system problem. The problem is that the workers are not getting the information they need.

Option 3: Incorrect. Surprising results are a symptom. They suggest that Terri is communicating an insufficient amount of information concerning her company's expectations.

Option 4: Correct. Surprising results are a sign that workers are not certain what is expected of them. This is an information problem.

Case Study: Question 2 of 3

Terri is trying to determine the reason for the problem with packaging the goods for transit. It isn't a constant problem. She thinks it might be caused by the company's "inspect and reinspect" packaging policy, an inconsistent supply of bubble wrap, or a misunderstanding among workers about packing standards. Which reason is the most likely cause, and why?

Options:

1. Because the performance is sometimes good, and sometimes poor, this indicates a lack of resources. The inconsistent supply of bubble wrap is the most likely cause.

2. Because the problem is intermittent, this indicates a lack of data. It's likely that the workers don't understand the packing standard.

3. The problem isn't constant, so it is probably caused by the company's "inspect and reinspect" packaging policy.

Answer

In fact, this is a resource problem, and is characterized by inconsistent supplies affecting performance.

Option 1: Correct. To identify the system problem that is causing production failures, Terri should examine the symptoms. Inconsistent performance is a sign of a resource problem.

Option 2: Incorrect. Erratic results indicate a lack of sufficient resources, not a lack of information.

Option 3: Incorrect. Inconsistent results are not the result of company procedures and policies, but are the result of insufficient resources.

Case Study: Question 3 of 3

Terri finds that goods are arriving late because they aren't being prepared for shipment on time. The slow production is causing cost overruns. Which of Terri's reasons is the most likely cause?

Options:

1. "Because this is a constant problem, the workers must not understand the packing efficiency standard."

2. "This might be caused by the company policy that requires each package to be inspected and reinspected by two workers."

3. "Because the goods are always late, the workers must need more efficient packaging materials."

Answer

In fact, slow production and cost overruns usually signal performance problems caused by policies and procedures.

Option 1: Incorrect. Work that is consistently late getting done is a sign of a system problem caused by company procedures and policies.

Option 2: Correct. Work that is behind schedule and causes cost overruns is a symptom of company policies and procedures that are impeding the work.

Option 3: Incorrect. A lack of resources, such as packing supplies, often results in either unfinished work or work that gets done in spurts, but it does not usually result in late work.

Terri should have recognized that a lack of data may be the source of the problem judging from the frequent requests for feedback and the unexpected excellence. Intermittent problems are often caused by inconsistent supplies. And inefficient policies and procedures often cause slow production and cost overruns.

Problem performance caused by the system is easy to miss. It is often blamed on workers. But if you investigate, and use the techniques explained in this topic, you may find that lack of data and inconsistent supplies are creating problems.

It is even easier to underestimate the negative impact of policies and procedures because they are designed specifically to improve performance. But remember that an inappropriate policy can dramatically limit performance.

Aptitude problems

Aptitude problems

According to the Merriam-Webster Dictionary, aptitude is "the natural ability" to perform a task. Aptitude problems stem from a problem with a worker's ability or a problem in the task.

Can you sing? Well, many people can sing, but can you become an opera singer? Opera singing requires more than a good voice. It requires you to sing in large halls, often in a different language, and as part of a dramatic presentation. To be an effective opera singer, you need the ability to sing as the operatic task demands.

Ability

Ability is the capacity, either innate or due to learning and practice, to perform a certain skill to a certain level.

Task

Task is the context in which the ability has to be demonstrated. Tasks will require different abilities and combinations of abilities.

Question

Patrick is aware that aptitude problems concern both the ability of a worker to perform the task, and the task itself. Help Patrick identify the corresponding characteristics of ability and task by matching each category to one or more problems.

Options:

A. ability
B. task

Targets:

1. particular context of performance
2. the capacity to perform a certain skill
3. requires different combinations of abilities
4. either innate or developed by learning and practice
5. the capacity to reach a certain level of skill

Answer

In fact, abilities, which may be physical or intellectual, are concerned with capacity, either innate or learned. Tasks involve the context of performance, which may require different combinations of abilities.

Abilities deal with what a person can do, but tasks deal with what a person does. Therefore, tasks must be viewed in a performance context.

Abilities concern what a person is capable of doing either mentally or physically. Therefore, the capacity to perform a skill is an ability, but the actual performance is a task.

Tasks must be performed within a particular context, and they often require more than one ability. Several abilities may be required to perform a single complex task.

While abilities can be either innate or learned, they can also be mental or physical. They deal with what a person is actually capable of doing.

Ability is all about a person's capacity to perform certain job tasks. If they are not capable of doing a job task, then they do not have the necessary ability.

Numerous abilities are relevant to the world of work. Not everyone has the same range of, or capacity for, abilities. Some abilities are more difficult to develop than others. This has a major impact on productivity and the remedies that you can apply to problem performance.

There are a number of key aspects of aptitude issues that affect the way you respond to problem performance.

Innateness

Is ability innate, or can it be learned? Some abilities are considered to be innate, or at least very difficult to learn. According to Malcolm Craig, these are color discrimination, visualization, rate control, general hearing, and originality.

If the ability is innate, or even difficult to learn, there may be nothing you can do to improve the worker's performance. You are therefore faced with accepting the performance level, or moving the worker to another task.

Dormancy

Most abilities need to be regularly used to enable proficiency. An obvious example is riding a bicycle. You may never forget how, but how proficient are you when you first return to riding a bicycle after a number of years of inactivity?

You can't expect employees to respond well to sudden performance demands if the ability hasn't been used for a while. Practice time must be offered when practical, or you must accept that performance will be poor at the restart of the task.

Ability task fit

Tasks may require different abilities or levels of ability. A worker may be asked to perform tasks above, or below, her existing ability level. If, after practice and support, her performance is still insufficient, there is an ability-task mismatch.

Match abilities to tasks. Accept that even with support and practice, some workers' ability levels will limit their performance. If they have more ability than needed, you should give workers more appropriate tasks.

Lucy and Simon have, what they think is, an aptitude problem in a member of their team. Follow their discussion as they establish the cause of their problem.

Lucy: Well, it took her a while to become confident but, with practice, she's quite competent at simple mathematical calculations. She had a job a few years ago that involved keeping account books.

Simon: So that's a case of dormant mathematical ability. But her problem with customers calling to change the layout of their designs is very different.

Lucy: The ability to visualize those layout changes is innate. There's very little we can do about that.

Simon: Well, it makes the decision a bit easier. We'll have to move her so she doesn't have to visualize design changes. We can put her in the invoicing section. Her mathematical abilities, after a bit of practice, might be good enough.

Problem Performance Management

Lucy: Are you sure? Some of the invoicing requires some pretty complicated mathematics. Is she up to that?

Simon: We'll find out. All we know so far is that she can manage simple mathematical reasoning. So we can give her a chance to improve her skill level, but if she doesn't succeed, we shouldn't perpetuate the problem by asking her to do a job she isn't able to do.

Case Study: Question 1 of 3
Scenario
Seebohm Brothers is a design company. Eric Seebohm calls you in as a consultant to help him resolve some problems he is having with the performance of some of his staff members.

Answer the questions to analyze the aptitude problems so as to identify appropriate responses.

Question
Eric tells you that he's worried about Claire, a member of his administrative staff. She can't seem to file the color-coded designs properly, although she's fine with alphabetical filing systems. Eric has shown her the simple system, but she still misfiles things. Which statements analyze the aptitude problem, and recommend an appropriate response?

Options:
1. Claire isn't using her reasoning ability to link the designs with the files.

2. Claire's problem could be that she can't discriminate between colors, which is an innate ability.

3. Eric should send Claire to an artistic course to improve her color discrimination.

4. Color discrimination is very difficult to develop, so Eric will have to change the system, or move Claire to a role that doesn't require that ability.

Answer

In fact, Claire's problem is most likely to be color discrimination, which is an innate ability. As such, it is very difficult to develop.

Option 1: Incorrect. Color discrimination is not a skill that requires reasoning. It is an innate ability. Option 2: Correct. An innate ability is one that a person is born with. It is very difficult, maybe

impossible, to learn. The ability to tell one color from another is a good example of an innate ability.

Option 3: Incorrect. The ability to distinguish between the colors in the color-coded designs is an innate ability. It is very difficult to learn, which makes it impractical to teach.

Option 4: Correct. Because color discrimination is an innate ability, it is unlikely that Claire will be able to learn it well enough to function satisfactorily where she is.

Case Study: Question 2 of 3

Eric also mentions his concerns about Dave, one of the designers. Dave is very creative, and is renowned for doing what he wants. Every year, Dave has problems following the rules and instructions about the layout of the company catalog. Which statements analyze the aptitude problem, and recommend an appropriate response?

Options:

1. If Dave only has to follow the rules annually, it's probably an issue of information ordering. Abilities need to be used regularly.

2. Eric needs to ask Dave to continually review the instructions on the layout of the company catalog while he's doing the job.

3. Dave can't be expected to show ability at information ordering. That's not an ability that designers are likely to have.

4. Information ordering is an innate ability. Eric will just have to accept that Dave is doing the best he can.

Answer

Actually, dormant abilities require time to reach proficiency. So Dave will have to review the instructions while he gets up to speed.

Option 1: Correct. This is an example of dormancy. This skill should be used more regularly to keep it sharp.

Option 2: Correct. Reviewing the instructions as he does the work will enable Dave to overcome the sluggish start that results from not practicing a skill for a long time.

Option 3: Incorrect. Information ordering is a skill that can be learned.

Option 4: Incorrect. Information ordering is not an example of an innate ability. This is an example of dormancy--a skill that needs to be used regularly to stay sharp.

Case Study: Question 3 of 3

Eric says he's also had problems with Sheena, who prices the goods in the catalog. She uses simple calculations in her everyday job, but she does not seem to grasp the multi-buy discounts, and trade purchase percentages featured in the catalog. Which statements analyze the aptitude problem, and recommend an appropriate response?

Options:

1. Eric can try to support Sheena, but if the peak of her mathematical reasoning has been reached, he may need to accept that her performance may not improve.

2. Sheena has demonstrated an ability with numbers, so this must be a temporary problem.

3. Eric should send Sheena to an accounting course. Then she's bound to become an expert.

4. The level of ability needed for the catalog pricing is different from the level that Sheena uses for her everyday work. Eric needs to match the abilities of the worker with the ones the task requires.

Answer

In fact, there must be a fit between the abilities the task requires, and the abilities the worker possesses. Otherwise, performance can be improved only to a certain extent.

Option 1: Correct. The ability level has to match the task. The tasks that Sheena can perform may be limited by her abilities.

Option 2: This is not an accurate analysis of Sheena's problem. Sheena has demonstrated her ability to perform simple calculations, but has had difficulties with more complex calculations. This is probably not a temporary problem.

Option 3: Incorrect. Eric's expectations for Sheena's abilities may be too high.

Option 4: Correct. If Sheena still struggles with the more complex tasks of catalog pricing even after she has received support and practice, Eric needs to accept that this task is above her ability level.

The issues at Seebohm Brothers demonstrate the problems that can be associated with aptitude. Claire's problem with color-coding is a lack of innate ability. Only a few abilities are clearly innate, but color discrimination is one of them. So there is little that can be done to improve Claire's ability with this task. Dave uses his information-ordering ability infrequently because most of the time he is encouraged to think freely without reference to rules and instructions. So his problem is one of practicing a dormant ability.

Sheena, on the other hand, does use mathematical reasoning regularly, so her problem is not likely to be one of dormancy. But the catalog requires a higher level of ability. She may, with support, develop to the required level, but she may not.

Aptitude problems need careful consideration. You should understand the ability of the worker and the ability the job requires, and match them. You should know that sometimes it will be difficult to improve a worker's ability.

Attitude problems

Attitude problems

How often have you heard that a worker who is not performing well has an attitude problem? It's one of the most common descriptions, and explanations, for problem performance at work. But using the brief description "attitude problem" may not be very useful.

You need to differentiate between the types of attitude problems if you are going to improve performance.

When people are accused of having attitude problems, it generally means that they can do the job, but are choosing not to. They have the relevant ability, and system problems are not the cause of problem performance, but they are still not performing adequately.

Job design

Salient factors in job design that affect attitude are concerned with challenging the worker to make full use of abilities and skills. This is related to the variety of skills used, and the autonomy of the worker. Unchallenging work negatively affects attitude, but too much challenge can demotivate.

Job value
How is the job valued within the rest of the company? A job that is considered to be without value will have a negative impact on the worker's self-esteem and attitude. Pay rates can be a crude measure of this, but fairness of pay is the most influential factor on attitude.

Supervisor interest
For many workers, a supervisor's interest in them is an important factor in defining attitude. This interest needs to be concerned with their personal welfare, as well as the technical aspects of their tasks.

Tim, Andrea, and Raymond are all considered to have attitude problems by their managers.

Tim: The work is just so boring. Every day, I'm doing the same old thing. I could do it in my sleep.

Andrea: I suppose I don't mind my job, but everyone in this company thinks my position doesn't provide an opportunity for advancement. Do you know I've been doing it for six years, and I'm still paid less than some of the trainees in other departments?

Raymond: I don't think this job is any worse than the others I've had, but my team leader doesn't seem to know I exist. I said I had a problem, and she said she'd come and talk about it. But she never did.

Question
Leon thinks that some of the people on his team have attitude problems. What workplace conditions could cause these problems?

Options:

1. the variety of skills required to perform the jobs
2. the intensity of work required by the jobs
3. how the pay compares to that of other jobs in the company
4. attention from supervisors
5. attention from colleagues

Answer

In fact, the conditions that create negative attitudes relate to job design, culture, and supervision.

Option 1: Correct. If a job is not challenging enough or is too challenging, employees will not stay engaged, and their attitude will suffer.

Option 2: Incorrect. Lack of variety, rather than intensity, can affect an employee's attitude towards work.

Option 3: Correct. The amount that workers get paid communicates to the workers how much their jobs are valued. If they do not feel valued, their attitude will be poor.

Option 4: Correct. There is a correlation between an employee's attitude and the quality of attention received from a supervisor. Employees like supervisors to care about their personal welfare, as well as job-related issues.

Option 5: Incorrect. There is no correlation between employees' attitudes and the attention they receive from their co-workers.

What can you do when faced with attitude problems?

Job design

Make work more challenging by increasing skill variety and autonomy. Consider rotating tasks among employees, and expanding tasks to include related procedures. Give workers choices in how, and when, they perform the tasks.

Job value

Problem Performance Management

Increase job profile without exaggerating importance. Arrange visits from senior managers. Minimize pay differences among similar jobs. Even negative attention, such as being berated, can have a short-term influence on attitude.

Supervisor interest

Instruct supervisors to interact with all employees. Regular, formal meetings with workers to discuss personal and work-related issues will help ensure this. Negative attitudes from supervisors can severely affect teams.

Case Study: Question 1 of 3

Scenario

Jason asks you to help him sort out the attitude problems on his team at SoftSync. The team has performed well in the past, but Jason feels that a negative attitude is developing, and it's having a negative effect on productivity.

In response to Jason's description of his problems, suggest techniques that will improve the attitude of his workers.

Question

Jason says that some of his team members are, at best, doing as little as possible to get the job done and, at worst, don't seem to care at all. They don't seem to find the work stimulating anymore. They seem to perform adequately with their own work, but the team's enthusiasm is gone. What pieces of advice should you give Jason to improve the attitude problems?

Options:

1. "I suggest you rotate duties among team members to give individual workers the challenge of doing different tasks."

2. "It sounds like they're too complacent. I'd let them know their jobs are on the line if their attitudes don't improve."

3. "They need something to revive their interest in the job. Take them back to the point when the job was challenging to them. A refresher course might work."

4. "You need to make the job more challenging so that your team members feel their abilities are fully utilized."

Answer

Actually, jobs need to be reasonably challenging, and rotating tasks is a simple way to give workers new challenges.

Option 1: Correct. Rotating jobs gives team members a new challenge. As long as that new challenge requires skills related to the ones team members already have, it will motivate them without discouraging and overwhelming them.

Option 2: Incorrect. A threat is a negative response that will only make negative attitudes worse.

Option 3: Incorrect. In order to add interest to their jobs, team members need a new challenge, rather than a refresher course.

Option 4: Correct. Employees get bored when they feel their skills aren't being used. Providing opportunities for more challenging work is motivating to employees.

Case Study: Question 2 of 3

The team members told Jason that they don't feel as important as the rest of the company. One worker told him that he didn't think anyone would notice if they didn't show up one day. What pieces of advice should you give Jason to improve this attitude problem?

Options:

Problem Performance Management

1. "Get senior management to pay a visit to the team, and take some interest in what's going on. That's positive attention."

2. "You've got to stop them from feeling devalued. This has affected their self-esteem, and caused the attitude problems."

3. "Tell them to do something that merits attention. That should provide some motivation."

4. "They will be valued when they learn to value themselves. So the remedy is in their own hands."

Answer

In fact, to make workers feel valued, senior managers should pay attention to all workers in the company.

Option 1: Correct. Attention from senior management would send the message that the team's work has been noticed and is valued.

Option 2: Correct. It is vital that all workers feel that the work they do is valued. If their work goes completely unnoticed, they will develop a poor attitude.

Option 3: Incorrect. The team members need to receive attention and recognition for the work they have already done.

Option 4: Incorrect. Until someone in authority pays attention to the work the team has done, team members will not know that their efforts are valued.

Case Study: Question 3 of 3

Jason tells you that he has to get this problem resolved because he doesn't have time to continue pursuing this with his team members. In what ways should you respond to this statement by Jason?

Options:

1. "The attitude of the supervisor is really important in establishing the attitude of the team."
2. "Good. You don't want to pay too much attention to them, or they'll think you don't trust them to handle the work on their own."
3. "Supervisors are key figures to the workers. So withdrawing your attention should encourage them to approach you more, and this will improve their general attitude."
4. "You should spend more time with them, not less, if you want to improve their attitudes. I'd suggest a regular schedule of individual meetings with each worker."

Answer

In fact, supervisors are key figures in determining the attitudes of their team members. Positive attention, on a regular basis, is the best approach.

Option 1: Correct. If Jason portrays a positive attitude about his work with the team and about the team itself, his attitude will be reflected by the team.

Option 2: Incorrect. If Jason does not regularly communicate about the team's achievements and contributions, team members will not know they are contributing in a meaningful way. This leads to a negative attitude.

Option 3: Incorrect. One key component for maintaining a positive attitude is giving the team consistent, positive feedback. Then team members will feel that their contribution is valued.

Option 4: Correct. Positive attention and interest from Jason will greatly affect the attitude of the employees. They will feel that their work is valued and that their contributions as employees are also valued.

Problem Performance Management

The attitudes of Jason's team members are partly the result of job design. Rotating tasks is one way to give workers a challenge. The team members also feel that they are unimportant to the company as a whole, and a simple remedy to this problem is to increase attention from senior management. But Jason is an equal and, arguably, a more vital influence on the team members. As their supervisor, he must provide positive attention if he wants team members to have good attitudes.

Attitude problems can be remedied. When you notice colleagues despairing about negative attitudes among their team members, advise them to make jobs more challenging, and ensure the team receives positive attention from managers.

Section 3 - Measuring Performance

In a study on performance management quoted in a white paper by the DDI Consultancy, 1,200 workers said they thought they could improve their daily output by at least 26 percent if they could remove some hindrances to performance.

And one in four said they could raise productivity by 50 percent. At the top of the list of hindrances was direction. This was followed by support and training. The workers wanted assistance in solving their performance problems.

Measuring performance starts with collecting data; otherwise it's like listening to tap dancers on the radio. You have no idea how well they are really performing.

Managers are busy people, but they must take the time to collect data on the performance of their staff members, or the performance management process is invalid. You may already have performance data for your staff members. Managers can use three techniques to collect data.

Assessing the standard of performance is an essential component of managing problem performance. If you want workers to improve, they must be able to understand not only where they are at the moment, but also where they are expected to be.

This means assessing their performance and giving them feedback on the shortfall between what they are producing now, and what they need to produce. Assessment is using performance data purposefully.

Managers informally appraise the performance of their workers all the time. But according to Paul Bernthal, citing research conducted by the DDI Consultancy, formal performance appraisal systems occur in 89 percent of organizations.

A performance appraisal system is a regular and formal pattern of assessment by a manager of the effectiveness of employees. It is:

- usually annual,
- frequently based on some form of rating system,
- sometimes used to appraise team performance, as well as individual performance.

Accurate, objective, and organized measurements of performance

Accurate, objective, and organized measurements of performance

In a study on performance management quoted in a white paper by the DDI Consultancy, 1,200 workers said they thought they could improve their daily output by at least 26 percent if they could remove some hindrances to performance.

And one in four said they could raise productivity by 50 percent. At the top of the list of hindrances was direction. This was followed by support and training. The workers wanted assistance in solving their performance problems.

More direction, support, and training stem from effective measurements of performance. If you were on Alan's team, think about how you would respond to this comment?

Problem Performance Management

Don't worry too much now about falling behind the others. I'm not sure why you can't keep up. But I'm sure you'll find a way around it eventually.

Alan won't make his employees feel very comfortable with this advice. They want accurate, objective, and organized measurements of their performance. Providing such measurements would allow Alan's employees to receive:

- clear direction about how to improve performance,
- tangible support,
- necessary training opportunities.

If you measure performance effectively, you will be able to provide your team with the benefits of direction, support, and training.

Question

Taylor advocates accurate, objective, and organized measurements of performance in his company. What benefits will this approach allow him to provide for his employees?

Options:

1. Employees will be provided with necessary training opportunities.

2. Workers will be given clear direction about how to improve performance.

3. Individuals will be encouraged to solve their own problems.

4. Staff members will be offered tangible support.

Answer

Actually, measuring performance effectively will allow Taylor to provide direction, support, and training.

Option 1: Correct. Taylor will be able to design specific and appropriate training interventions that effectively meet the needs of his employees.

Option 2: Correct. With clear direction, employees will not be confused about the actions they should take. They will be more motivated because they clearly understand their responsibilities.

Option 3: Incorrect. Employees may need to learn to solve some problems by themselves, but the benefits of effective measurement of performance include support, clear direction, and appropriate training interventions.

Option 4: Correct. When Taylor's employees are given proper support, a feeling of empowerment and increased motivation for positive change will result.

Measure the performance of your team members effectively, and you will manage their performance effectively.

Techniques to collect data on performance

Techniques to collect data on performance

Measuring performance starts with collecting data; otherwise it's like listening to tap dancers on the radio. You have no idea how well they are really performing.

Managers are busy people, but they must take the time to collect data on the performance of their staff members, or the performance management process is invalid. You may already have performance data for your staff members. Managers can use three techniques to collect data.

Direct observation

A manager using direct observation sets aside specific times to work alongside workers, or just stands back and notes performance. The manager may choose to do this in relation to a specific activity.

Customer and colleagues

Data can be collected from customers and colleagues. You need to decide if you are actively seeking the data, or whether you will rely on unsolicited information. Data can be collected from actual customers or "mystery customers."

Self-assessment

Self-assessment involves asking workers to identify their own good and bad performance. Critical incident reporting techniques, supported by a self-rating system, work well.

Different managers collect data in different ways.

Judy

Judy spends one day a month working alongside each of her workers on the sales floor. Even though her staff members know she is assessing them, they find it tremendously supportive, and Judy can help them with direct feedback about what she sees.

Damon

Damon has mystery customers--researchers acting as customers--make phone calls to his help desk team. The researchers pose problems that require detailed technical help. They collect data on the quality of the technical support offered and the workers' interpersonal skills.

Skip

Skip uses self-assessment by meeting with his team quarterly. His workers are expected to bring summaries of the work they have completed with each client, as well as plans for future work. Skip can then refer back to past meetings to discuss how workers have performed against the plans.

Question

Problem Performance Management

Joe feels that he knows exactly how his team members perform, even though he works in a different building. Which statements describe the techniques that he should use to collect performance data?

Options:

1. collating all customer thank-you and complaint letters for each employee
2. asking his team members to role-play difficult customers with each other so he can collect data on their performance
3. working alongside each staff member on a regular basis
4. asking staff members to rate their performance on a scale from one to five
5. asking staff members to assess their colleagues in a public meeting

Answer

Actually, Joe should use direct observation, customer feedback, and self-assessment as data collection techniques.

Option 1: Correct. This is a great way for Joe to collect data on how colleagues and customers perceive an employee. This data can be used to measure an employee's performance

Option 2: Incorrect. Joe needs to directly observe his employees in the actual working environment to evaluate their job performance.

Option 3: Correct. Direct observation such as this will allow Joe to show support for his team members and give direct feedback concerning their performance.

Option 4: Correct. Keeping records of employees' self-assessments allows Joe to refer back to previous meetings to determine how workers have performed relative to plans that were previously set.

Option 5: Incorrect. Feedback from colleagues and customers should be gathered in a confidential manner.

Certain factors regarding the way these techniques are applied in the workplace must be taken into account.

Contextual factors

Consider the external, contextual factors that could affect performance. For example, resources and customer attitude may limit performance. Observe on more than one occasion, or the data are insufficient.

Unsolicited data

Unsolicited data often only relate to exceptional performance. Check the data, and use other sources whenever possible to ensure lack of bias. Be consistent in seeking comments from colleagues. Do not just apply this to problem performers.

Exercise judgment

You need to exercise judgment about interpreting what people say about themselves. Most people think they do a good job, but some are reluctant to say so. Many people have a tendency to be critical of themselves.

Case Study: Question 1 of 3

Scenario

You have been asked to collect some performance data on your team members. How will you do this? You begin with Sharon, who is a very anxious team member.

Answer the questions concerning members of your team to use effective techniques for data collection.

Question

Problem Performance Management

You observe Sharon at work one day, and notice some problems with the way she responds to irate customers. What should you do?

Options:

1. I'm going to repeat the observation, because one set of data, good or bad, is insufficient.

2. I'll accept the data as a good indication of Sharon's performance.

3. I'll work alongside Sharon as another way of collecting data on performance.

4. Because there was a problem, I'll observe Sharon again.

Answer

In fact, direct observation must be repeated for comparative purposes, and to ensure that unusual circumstances have not affected the performance. Working alongside the employee is a sensible alternative method of collecting data.

Option 1: Correct. Comparative data is required for a more accurate result.

Option 2: Incorrect. Data taken from only one observation lacks validity.

Option 3: Correct. Your data will be more accurate if it comes from multiple sources.

Option 4: Incorrect. Another observation is required, not because of the problem, but to ensure accuracy.

Case Study: Question 2 of 3

Tonya has received the most unsolicited praise from customers in the entire company. How should you respond to this information in applying effective data collection techniques?

Options:

1. I'll only use customer feedback to check on problem performers.

2. Unsolicited comments tend to focus on exceptional circumstances. I'll check with customers directly.

3. If customers have commented favorably of their own volition, Tonya must be an exceptionally good performer.

4. I'll check with more than one customer to ensure there wasn't any bias in the unsolicited comments received.

Answer

Actually, customer feedback is useful data when verified on more than one occasion. Unsolicited data tend to relate to exceptional events.

Option 1: Incorrect. Customer feedback can be a reliable source of information. It should be sought directly to avoid relying only on unsolicited feedback.

Option 2: Correct. Getting direct customer feedback will generate more reliable results.

Option 3: Incorrect. Information will be more accurate if comparative data is used.

Option 4: Correct. Comparative data is always more accurate.

Case Study: Question 3 of 3

You ask Jim to provide you with a self-assessment of his performance in the past six months. He rates his performance as generally poor, but all other data indicate he's a good worker. How would you respond?

Options:

1. I'll exercise careful judgment about the self-assessment. Some people can be overly self-critical.

2. Jim may be reluctant to praise himself, even when he really thinks he has performed well.

3. Jim knows his own performance better than anyone else. This is more significant than the other data.

4. If Jim had said he performed better than indicated by the other data, I would discount his self-assessment.

Answer

Actually, self-assessment gives data that you must examine closely. People are reluctant to praise themselves too highly, and can be more critical of themselves than they would be of other people in the same circumstances.

Option 1: Correct. Collecting self-assessment data does require the use of good judgment. The results can be biased.

Option 2: Correct. Most people are reticent to identify their own achievements. For this reason, self- assessment data requires extra judgment.

Option 3: Incorrect. Self-assessment data needs careful interpretation because most people are reluctant to praise their own behavior.

Option 4: Incorrect. Self-assessment data can be complicated. This is why comparative data is helpful. Sometimes self-assessment data needs to be carefully considered and interpreted.

So data collection by direct observation and from colleagues and customers should be repeated for comparative purposes, and to avoid contextual anomalies. Self-assessed data require cautious interpretation.

Collecting data on performance is an essential, but time-consuming, business. Many managers will be tempted to skimp on the process, and will end up with inaccurate and unverified data. From this inauspicious start, the process of performance management never recovers.

Sorin Dumitrascu

You now have the tools to make data collection on performance in your organization a manageable and effective process.

Standards of performance

Standards of performance

Assessing the standard of performance is an essential component of managing problem performance. If you want workers to improve, they must be able to understand not only where they are at the moment, but also where they are expected to be.

This means assessing their performance and giving them feedback on the shortfall between what they are producing now, and what they need to produce. Assessment is using performance data purposefully.

To assess standards of performance effectively, you will need to incorporate three factors in the design of the assessment process. You must be clear about what aspect of performance you are assessing. You must assess with a purpose, and you must make the assessment objective and meaningful.

Outcomes

Measure outcome, rather than behavior. Be concerned with effectiveness, rather than actions. Within legal and ethical standards, does it matter how people behave as long as they produce results?

Objectivity

The assessment should be criterion-referenced, not norm-referenced. Use measures that are generally applicable standards, not standards based merely on comparisons within teams, or between individuals.

Gaps

Concentrate on something specific--the gap between current performance and expected performance. This creates a tangible, realistic measure that allows you to identify the level of performance improvement required.

These are some examples of effective assessment strategies that incorporate the factors of outcomes, objectivity, and measurement in their designs.

Complex Computing Inc.

Some people thought Lucy was too slow at programming. But her manager found that she finished on time. Lucy spent more time on preparation than her colleagues, and therefore had fewer problems to sort out. Measuring her on outcome, not behavior, was the key.

Price Howard

Larry's dispatch team was coasting along and performing better than the other teams. But when the company hired a consultant, she pointed out that, by national standards, the team was only average. So now it has to improve.

Delion Air

Ron's performance stayed constant, even though his previous manager told him that the customer reports were

Problem Performance Management

unsatisfactory. When Lauren became his manager, she told him that he was not giving the passengers hourly updates on arrival times, as was expected of him. Now customers rate him highly.

Question

Danielle was asked to design an effective assessment procedure for the company performance management program. What factors should she take into account in the design?

Options:

1. The system she designs must be norm-referenced.
2. She should ensure that it concentrates on outcomes, not behavior.
3. Behavioral measures are preferential to measures of outcome.
4. She needs to build in a comparison of current, and expected, performance levels.
5. She must design a criterion-referenced system.

Answer

Actually, the system should be outcome-based, incorporating a measure of the performance gap. Criterion-referenced systems are more effective than norm-referenced systems.

Option 1: Incorrect. It is more accurate and effective to compare employee performance to an established standard than to compare it to the performance of other employees.

Option 2: Correct. By focusing on outcomes, Danielle can ensure objectivity, because she will be focusing on results instead of outstanding behaviors.

Option 3: Incorrect. Because the goal is to improve the outcome, it is better to measure actual outcome than to measure behavior. Sometimes when behavior seems problematic, the employee is actually producing acceptable results.

Option 4: Correct. This effectively enables employees to SEE where they stand in relation to Danielle's expectations.

Option 5: Correct. A criterion-referenced system is an effective system where an employees performance is compared with an established standard--but not with the performance of fellow employees. This keeps the assessment objective

How can you use the factors to design effective assessments in the real world of work? You need to ensure that standards are derived from performance outcomes, not behavior. When performance is compared with meaningful, external criteria, the performance gap should be evident.

Outcomes

Avoid measuring behavior. Instead, identify the outcome that is required. Defining the desired outcome, but not prematurely assessing the process of achieving it, is essential.

Objectivity

Use an objective assessment process that removes distractions based on the individual involved. Beware of assuming that performance in one context carries over to another, and also of overvaluing more recent events.

Gaps

The performance gap between expected, and delivered, results should be broken down into a prioritized list of required performance improvements in relation to the overall outcomes defined for the task.

Problem Performance Management

Case Study: Question 1 of 3
Scenario

You are assessing the performance of George, one of your lathe setter/operators. George is new to the team, and has impressed everybody. He is by far the quickest machine setter that you have ever employed. But you are aware that his bearing production is below target.

Answer the questions to show how to effectively assess George's performance.

Question

How would you assess George's speed at setting up the lathes, and set his production target?

Options:

1. The setting-up figures are concerned with behavior. I want to assess George's performance in terms of outcome.

2. George's above-average lathe-setting speed would obviously indicate that he is capable of higher production figures.

3. George is an above-average setter/operator because he has such expertise at setting up the machines.

4. I would assess George's performance based on his below-target outcome figures for bearing production.

Answer

In fact, you need to assess George on outcomes, not on behavior.

Option 1: Correct. The company's goal is to improve the employees' production or outcome. That is why it is more effective for you to assess George's outcomes, rather than individual behaviors.

Option 2: Incorrect. Assessing behaviors instead of outcomes can lead to misleading conclusions.

Option 3: Incorrect. While it is true that George is a fast machine setter, a productive assessment that will lead to a realization of company goals requires that you only assess his outcomes.

Option 4: Correct. George's outcomes should be assessed, and then the desired production level should be established.

Case Study: Question 2 of 3

George's performance figures are just above average for the team, but below target. The production target is based on figures from across the industry, and relates to comparative production situations. How would you use this information in your assessment of George's performance?

Options:

1. The key figure is the team average. Norm-based criteria are the most effective assessment vehicle.

2. I would revise the target figures to relate more specifically to the team's actual production.

3. George's performance assessment must be criterion-based, using external, objective standards of performance.

4. My assessment is that George is underperforming. His comparison with the team is less significant than his failure to meet the production target.

Answer

Actually, using criterion-based assessment ensures objectivity.

Option 1: Incorrect. Norm-based criteria can be misleading. Criteria-based assessment offers a larger basis for comparison.

Option 2: Incorrect. Instead of changing the goal, establish the performance level--and allow employees to improve their performance to meet it.

Option 3: Correct. The assessment will be more reliable if it is based on established criteria from across the industry.

Option 4: Correct. Because you are using a criterion-based assessment rather than a norm-based one, George is underperforming.

Case Study: Question 3 of 3

The target for bearing production is 30 trays per day accepted by quality control. George produces an average of 35 trays, but only 25 of them are accepted. How would you respond to this information?

Options:

1. George needs to work more slowly and carefully.

2. George's actual production figures of an average of 25 trays per day demonstrate the performance gap.

3. The first thing George must do is speak to quality control to find out what is wrong with his bearings.

4. I would tell George to prioritize reducing the number of defective bearings he produces as the first way to bridge the performance gap.

Answer

In fact, you must identify the performance gap in terms of outcomes, not behavior. Then you can use this information to prioritize actions to bridge the gap.

Option 1: Incorrect. It is not effective to focus on assessing or modifying behavior. By concentrating on outcomes and performance gaps, George can set well-defined goals and work towards meeting them.

Option 2: Correct. The performance gap is the difference between the target of 30 trays per day and George's actual outcome of 25 trays per day. This gap defines the goal for improvement.

Option 3: Incorrect. After the performance gap is assessed, then the results should be broken down into a prioritized list of required improvements.

Option 4: Correct. Informing George of the gap and then supporting him in making the needed improvements is an effective way to improve his production.

Effective assessment must concentrate on outcomes, not behavior, and compare the outcomes to criterion-based targets. This will help to identify ways of prioritizing developments to bridge the performance gap.

Assessing standards is a facet of problem performance that must be managed effectively if you are going to be successful in improving performance.

Best practices in performance appraisal systems

Best practices in performance appraisal systems

Managers informally appraise the performance of their workers all the time. But according to Paul Bernthal, citing research conducted by the DDI Consultancy, formal performance appraisal systems occur in 89 percent of organizations.

A performance appraisal system is a regular and formal pattern of assessment by a manager of the effectiveness of employees. It is:

- usually annual,
- frequently based on some form of rating system,
- sometimes used to appraise team performance, as well as individual performance.

Lawrence Kleiman, quoted in the Encyclopedia of Management, states that: "One study found that a majority of companies (65 percent) are dissatisfied with their performance appraisal systems." So what characterizes effective appraisal systems? In another DDI white paper, Roger Sumlin, Paul Bernthal, and colleagues used a variety of studies to identify the characteristics that differentiate a highly effective system from a less effective one.

Alignment

The most critical effectiveness factor was whether performance management supported organizational goals and was integrated with other systems. Alignment was the least common quality found in the studies they examined.

Simplicity

Effective systems were flexible, simple to use, and easy to understand. The systems were simple enough to be integrated into the daily work process. Simplicity fostered faster acceptance by the workforce.

Rigor

The most successful performance management systems required training in using the system, established clear accountability for the people using it, and focused on competencies.

Senior management

Senior managers have a direct influence on the effectiveness of the system, depending on their personal participation. It is essential that they ensure that people who report to them are also effective in their implementation of the system.

Does your organization have an effective performance appraisal system?

Although it is possible to identify good practice in performance appraisal, it isn't always as evident as it should be in many organizations.

Problem Performance Management

Select each company for some examples of what they have done to devise effective performance appraisal systems.

Spacework

Spacework has an environmental procedure to increase the use of recyclable materials. Its appraisal system includes this factor in the rating system used for all workers. Its ethical policy links environmental stewardship and good performance.

Tetral

A committee of workers from all divisions and grades designed Tetral's appraisal system. It is a straightforward rating approach based on production figures already generated for bonus payments. Workers verify the rating at annual reviews.

Dispatchfast

Dispatchfast offers a brief annual refresher training program for all staff and managers. Duties and responsibilities for completing and processing documentation are covered, as well as the appeals procedure. The company sees preparation as key to success.

Wisharts

Consultants pointed to the time when the CEO at Wisharts publicly rebuked a director for failing to complete his subordinate's appraisal as a "highly influential episode." In their words, "This event stamped the significance of the appraisal system on everyone's mind."

Question

Paula has been asked to develop a performance appraisal system for her company. What practices should she incorporate to make her appraisal system most effective?

Options:

1. She should ensure that the system is based on clear accountability by the people using it.

2. She should design a system that is informal.

3. She should align the appraisal system to support organizational goals.

4. Paula should insist that senior managers are visibly using the system.

5. Paula should create a flexible and simple system.

Answer

In fact, an effective appraisal system is aligned to organizational goals. It is simple to use, and is implemented rigorously with support from senior management.

Option 1: Correct. A system can only be rigorous if those who use it are properly trained and are held accountable for their resulting performance.

Option 2: Incorrect. An appraisal system needs to be simple, but it also needs to be formal enough to be taken seriously.

Option 3: Correct. An effective appraisal system is aligned with organizational goals. This alignment gives the appraisal system more credibility.

Option 4: Correct. Employees are more likely to believe that an appraisal system is important if it is used by senior management.

Option 5: Correct. An appraisal system that is user-friendly is more likely to be accepted by the workforce than a system that is difficult to administer and understand.

Problem Performance Management

Many organizations struggle to create an effective performance appraisal system. Now you know the characteristics that determine the success of the system, so you can use them effectively.

CHAPTER 3 - Problem Performance Improvement

CHAPTER 3 - Problem Performance Improvement

Section 1 - Counseling
Section 2 - Supporting Improvement
Section 3 - Changing the Work Situation

Section 1 - Counseling
Section 1 - Counseling

"Termination" is at the end of the range of responses to problem performance, and "Disciplinary Procedures" is in the middle. "Counseling," the first step to helping workers improve their effectiveness, begins the process.

Many managers find it difficult to inform a worker that he is a problem performer. They may avoid the issue as much as possible, or they may overreact to the situation. Here are some examples of managers informing subordinates that they have performance problems.

To make performance improvements happen, you need a clear and deliberate procedure--usually referred to as a performance improvement plan. An effective performance improvement plan has three major components.

Performance problems are usually related to work, but sometimes problems are caused by other issues in the worker's life. You must establish the best way to handle this sort of problem.

Counseling workers to improve performance

Controversial issues

"Termination" is at the end of the range of responses to problem performance, and "Disciplinary Procedures" is in the middle. "Counseling," the first step to helping workers improve their effectiveness, begins the process.

Some people see counseling as an endless discussion that leads nowhere, but this is not the approach advocated here. Counseling is an approach characterized by:
- ownership,
- methodical planning,
- a recognition of its limitations.

The counseling approach is beneficial because it:
- enables workers to own their performance problems,
- uses methodical planning to achieve improvement,

- - encourages workers to access external specialist support when necessary.

At Truck Training, the counseling approach has been used to help a variety of workers improve their performance.

Nathan

Nathan is a sensitive guy who reacts badly to what he sees as criticism, so his supervisor avoided talking to him about the customer complaints. Nathan was ignorant of the problem until his manager carefully informed him about the complaints. Now Nathan accepts his problem, and is working on it.

Maggie

Maggie struggled with organizing the drivers' shifts. Everyone knew about it, and it had become a joke. But it became less funny when she didn't improve. Maggie and her manager produced a clear, organized plan, and the improvements were evident immediately.

Julie

Julie's attendance record was awful. Her manager pleaded with her, and finally threatened her, to no effect. Then she realized that Julie's problem was more than just poor attendance. Julie's alcohol problem required expert support from an external agency.

Nathan needed to take ownership of his problem before he could address it. Maggie failed to benefit from a lot of good humor and little organization. It took a rigorous performance improvement plan to head her in the right direction. Julie was failing at work because her problems were much bigger than work problems. It took more expertise than anyone at Truck Training had to get her back on the right track.

Question

Dennis strongly advocated counseling workers as the first stage to improving their performance. Which statements describe the benefits of counseling?

Options:

1. Counseling uses methodical planning to achieve improvement.

2. Counseling uses discussion to support workers.

3. Counseling enables workers to own their performance problem.

4. Counseling encourages workers to access external specialist support when necessary.

5. Counseling avoids termination of employees.

Answer

Actually, the benefits of counseling are ownership of the problem performance, methodical planning to achieve improvement, and access to external support agencies.

Option 1: Correct. Counseling can be used to produce a clear, organized plan, leading to immediate improvements.

Option 2: Incorrect. Counseling that uses discussion is not the type of counseling discussed in this lesson that leads to immediate positive results.

Option 3: Correct. One of the benefits of the counseling approach is that it enables workers to feel responsibility for their problems and have control over solving those problems.

Option 4: Correct. Sometimes an employee's problems are much bigger than work problems. When additional expertise is required, counseling can direct an employee to the needed outside source of support.

Problem Performance Management

Option 5: Incorrect. Counseling cannot guarantee that an employee will make the necessary improvements to avoid termination. The employee still has the power to make choices.

Counseling workers is the first stage in improving their problem performance.

Techniques to effectively inform a worker of problem

performance

Techniques to effectively inform a worker of problem performance

Many managers find it difficult to inform a worker that he is a problem performer. They may avoid the issue as much as possible, or they may overreact to the situation. Here are some examples of managers informing subordinates that they have performance problems.

Ashley

"I know you're busy. This is ridiculous, but I've got to talk to you about a customer complaint. A few weeks ago, I received a call from an irate customer, but I forgot to pass it on. So watch what you say to customers, will you?"

Will

"Listen. I've been told that you haven't been keeping up with your replies to customer inquiries. I've told you before, you have to reply within 48 hours. Now make sure you do in the future, or else you're in big trouble."

Kashuo

"Dermot, you've really messed up again. The photocopier is out of paper. And don't tell me that it's not your job! It's your problem--figure it out. Don't come complaining to me about being busy. Get on with it!"

Eve

"I'd like to meet with you today to talk about a customer complaint. We need to discuss what happened, and see if there's anything we need to do about it. Then, if I need to, I can make sure that you're following the procedures correctly."

Ashley finally spoke to his subordinate when he had time, and tried to deal with a problem he could hardly remember. Will focused on reprimanding his team member, and Kashuo made sure that his worker knew that he was at fault. But Eve informed her subordinate much more effectively.

1. Preparation

Eve did not approach informing her subordinate as a spontaneous, casual conversation. She recognized that such a discussion may lead to further actions, and needs to be effectively planned.

2. Purpose

Eve knew what she was trying to achieve by informing her subordinate of the problem performance. She didn't use a punitive approach. It was the beginning of the process of supporting that worker to improve performance.

3. Style

Eve was calm and considered in her style. She was not anxious about having to tell her subordinate that there was a problem. She was direct, firm, and positive. She reassured the worker that this was a mutual problem that she was going to help to remedy.

Question

Ron had worked really hard to make sure that, as a manager, he could effectively inform a staff member of her problem performance. Which approaches do you think he used to inform his staff member?

Options:

1. He was spontaneous, and talked to his staff member when he could.

2. He planned and prepared for meetings with his staff member.

3. He reprimanded his employee.

4. He was supportive of that worker to improve her performance.

5. He reassured his worker that the problem was a shared one.

Answer

In fact, the best approach to informing workers about problem performance includes planning and preparation, being supportive, and describing the problem as a mutual one.

Option 1: Incorrect. A discussion of problem performance needs to be well planned, not spontaneous, to be productive.

Option 2: Correct. Ron recognized that such a discussion may lead to further actions, and needs to be effectively planned.

Option 3: Incorrect. Taking a punitive approach, such as a reprimand, will lead to resentment and may destroy any chance of working together with the employee to solve the problem.

Option 4: Correct. If Ron keeps in mind what he wants to achieve with the meeting, he will be supportive of that worker in order to improve performance.

Option 5: Correct. Ron needed to be direct, firm, and reassure the worker that this was a mutual problem that he was going to help to remedy.

By using the techniques, you will ensure that you are effective in informing workers of problem performance.

Preparation

Choose a private place, and ensure that you have enough time. Inform the worker at an early stage, not when the behavior is established, and schedule the meeting as close to an incident as possible. Record the discussion.

Purpose

Make clear statements about the reason for informing the worker about the problem. Identify the ways that support will be offered, and the consequences if there is no improvement in performance.

Style

Describe the problem as a mutual one. Adopt a light, firm tone, and listen to the worker's explanation of the problem and remedy. Seek agreement, but insist on certain actions by the worker or the worker may not accept responsibility.

Case Study: Question 1 of 3
Scenario

You need to tell Neil that his work on the help desk is unsatisfactory. Members of the sales department have complained that Neil gave them poor instructions. They have been unable to use the customer database for a mail merge to send out some important letters.

Demonstrate how you will inform Neil of the problem by answering the questions in order.

Question

You are meeting Neil and a couple of other colleagues for coffee. What will you say to him about the problem?

Options:

1. "I want to talk about the sales department. We have a few minutes now, don't we?"

2. "Can we meet later today in my office to talk about your advice to the sales department?"

3. "An issue about your advice to the sales department has come up. Can we schedule a meeting in the next week or two?"

4. "I set aside an hour to spend with you on this."

Answer

Actually, you need to schedule a private meeting with Neil, and allocate enough time to it.

Option 1: Incorrect. The meeting needs to be well planned and prepared for. Choose a private place and ensure that you have enough time.

Option 2: Correct. This meeting is planned and prepared for, and will be private. The employee knows what to expect and can also come prepared.

Option 3: Incorrect. It is important to inform the worker at an early stage, not when the behavior is established, and to schedule the meeting as close to an incident as possible

Option 4: Correct. You must ensure that you have scheduled enough time for an effective meeting that does not feel rushed for you or the employee.

Case Study: Question 2 of 3

You meet with Neil in your office later on that day. How will you inform him about his problem performance?

Options:

1. "I want to meet with you because you have given incorrect advice to the sales department about how to mail merge."

2. "If you give wrong instructions to users, then I will have to consider taking you off the help desk."

3. "I wanted to talk with you about your performance on the help desk."

4. "This is quite an important issue, you know. If it happens again, it could cause a lot of bad feeling between us and the sales department."

Answer

In fact, you must explain the reason for the meeting, and ensure that Neil understands the consequences if he doesn't improve his performance.

Option 1: Correct. You need to make clear statements about the problem and the reason for informing the worker about the problem.

Option 2: Correct. The employee needs to be informed of the consequences if there is no improvement in performance.

Option 3: Incorrect. It is better to be direct and clear in telling the employee why you need to talk to him about the problem performance.

Option 4: Incorrect. It is vital for a successful resolution that the consequences of the problem performance are clearly stated to the employee.

Case Study: Question 3 of 3

You continue the discussion with Neil, and he says that he doesn't have time to research mail merges. He suggests that he should forward all queries about mail merges to other colleagues. How will you respond to him?

Options:

1. "I will personally make sure that you have the time to complete all the research on mail merges that you need."

2. "It's your responsibility to know all about these programs. You will have to find the time."

3. "I'm not sure that's the right solution. But if you insist, I suppose I'll have to go along with it."

4. "No. I can't agree with that. Your job entails giving effective instructions on how to set up a mail merge."

Answer

In fact, you need to adopt a firm but light tone, and listen to Neil. However, if you disagree, you must insist on the right course of action.

Option 1: Correct. It is most effective to describe the problem as a mutual one, and give your support to the employee's efforts to improve.

Option 2: Incorrect. You need to offer to support the employee's efforts to solve the problem.

Option 3: Incorrect. You must maintain a firm tone and insist on the needed performance level, but offer support.

Option 4: Correct. It is best to seek agreement, but you must insist on certain actions by the worker, or the worker may not accept responsibility.

Problem Performance Management

To inform one of your staff members that he has a problem with some aspect of his performance, you need to prepare and consider carefully when and where you speak to him. You must establish the purpose of the discussion, and the consequences if he cannot improve his behavior. Throughout the discussion, you need to be firm with him. But make sure you listen to him, and if you disagree, do not be afraid to insist on a plan of action.

If you follow these simple techniques, you can establish an effective and purposeful way of informing your workers about performance problems.

An effective performance improvement plan

An effective performance improvement plan

To make performance improvements happen, you need a clear and deliberate procedure--usually referred to as a performance improvement plan. An effective performance improvement plan has three major components.

A gap statement

A gap statement measures the difference between desired and actual performance. This gap must be stated in measurable terms, with supporting evidence. It must relate clearly to the job expectations as understood by the worker.

An activity profile

An activity profile must state what actions the manager, and other members of the organization, will undertake to help workers improve their performance. The actions to be taken by the workers must also be explicitly stated.

An improvement period

Problem Performance Management

The period over which the improvement should take place must be indicated clearly. There must be an end date when performance will be measured again, using the same criteria that indicated a performance gap. The period allowed must take into account any factors like vacations.

Question

Dennis has been asked to design a procedure for developing performance improvement plans throughout the company. Which essential components must Dennis include?

Options:

1. the time by which the improvement must be shown
2. a statement about the involvement of the human resources department in developing the plans
3. a statement that measures the difference between desired and actual performance
4. a clause accepting blame, signed by the worker
5. the actions that all personnel in the organization must take to support the improvement of performance

Answer

Actually, performance improvement plans must identify the performance gap, signify the actions that all personnel must take to make the plan work, and specify the performance improvement period.

Option 1: Correct. There must be an end date when performance will be measured again, using the same criteria that indicated a performance gap.

Option 2: Incorrect. This is not an essential component of a performance improvement plan because the human resources department is not involved in the development of each plan.

Option 3: Correct. This is called a gap statement. It must be stated in measurable terms, with supporting evidence and the employee must understand how it relates to job expectations.

Option 4: Incorrect. This is not a necessary part of a performance improvement plan because this type of plan is not about placing blame; it is about making improvements.

Option 5: Correct. An activity profile must state what actions the manager, other members of the organization, and the workers will undertake to help improve their performance.

The most effective performance improvement plans are not imposed by managers on their workers-- they are the products of both parties working together. And plans that motivate can be easier to see through to fruition. As a manager, you should use some essential techniques to develop performance improvement plans.

The Gap Statement

You need to provide irrefutable evidence of the performance gap, and ensure that workers truly accept their responsibility. Any factors that might have limited performance must be acknowledged.

The Activity Profile

To make the activity profile effective, you will need to order the activities by prioritizing them against organizational objectives. Some activities will produce immediate improvements, which may help a worker's self-esteem.

The Improvement Period

This should be a jointly agreed on schedule that accepts phased improvement. This time is best supported by periodic reviews, which can help to motivate workers faced with lengthy and demanding schedules.

Case Study: Question 1 of 3

Scenario

Tania is responsible for sending an acknowledgement of a customer complaint within three working days. Then she has to investigate the complaint in the relevant department, and reply to the customer with her findings within 15 working days.

However, Tania has not replied to customer complaints within the allotted time period.

Show how you will develop a performance improvement plan to remedy the problem by answering the questions in order.

Question

Tania tells you that the problem has been greatly exaggerated. She has only been late with a couple of the letters, and this occurred because of a lack of cooperation from the departments when she investigated the complaint. Which replies would be most appropriate?

Options:

1. "Oh, come on! I bet it's more than a couple of letters."

2. "I know that you have been late with six acknowledgement letters and four findings letters in the past month."

3. "OK, if it's the fault of other departments, you could have informed me, and I would have written to the customers."

4. "The responsibility for the letters is still yours. Even if the departments were difficult, you have to reply to the customer within the allotted time periods."

Answer

In fact, you need to provide irrefutable evidence of the performance gap, and ensure that Tania accepts her responsibility for the problem.

Option 1: Incorrect. You need specific evidence of the performance gap.

Option 2: Correct. By providing irrefutable evidence of the performance gap, you ensure that workers

truly accept their responsibility. Specific facts without accusations make the best evidence.

Option 3: Incorrect. It is good to acknowledge the factors that were interfering with Tania's performance, but it is vital to maintain that the worker is responsible for her own work performance.

Option 4: Correct. You acknowledged the difficult departments that limited performance, but you maintained that Tania is responsible for her own work performance.

Case Study: Question 2 of 3

Which actions would you suggest to Tania to remedy the problem?

Options:

1. "Our customer charter defines that we will investigate and reply within 15 days, so that letter must go out on time. We can worry about the acknowledgement letters afterward."

2. "We have to acknowledge the complaint. It's bad manners not to, and customers will be angry."

3. "To speed up your investigations, I'm arranging for you to connect with the department head and not to go to each staff member concerned."

Problem Performance Management

4. "We should be able to arrange some meetings with department heads in the foreseeable future. If you get their support, your investigations should be easier."

Answer

Actually, you need to prioritize an action plan against company objectives, and try to build in some immediate results.

Option 1: Correct. To make the activity profile effective, you will need to order the activities by prioritizing them against organizational objectives. It is an organizational objective to investigate and reply within 15 days.

Option 2: Incorrect. The decision about which activities to pursue should be based on prioritization and your company's objectives.

Option 3: Correct. This activity will produce immediate improvements, which may boost Tania's confidence and encourage her to improve her performance even more.

Option 4: Incorrect. Activities which produce immediate improvements should receive a high priority.

Case Study: Question 3 of 3

Tania suggests that she should take the next complaint letter directly to the department head concerned. How should you reply to this suggestion?

Options:

1. "Good idea. I agree, it will work much better if we have an actual complaint to focus on."

2. "I think that we should review your experiences after you have dealt with some complaints, starting with the department heads."

3. "I'm going to arrange a meeting right now with the department heads. I don't think we gain anything from waiting for the actual complaints."

4. "Once we've set that system up, we should be able to forget about that problem forever."

Answer

Actually, an improvement plan should have a jointly set timetable and include phased improvements and periodic reviews.

Option 1: Correct. This should be a jointly agreed-on schedule that accepts phased improvement.

Option 2: Correct. This time is best supported by periodic reviews of Tania's work.

Option 3: Incorrect. This schedule of measuring improvement should be mutually agreed on; not decided by you alone.

Option 4: Incorrect. This time is best supported by periodic reviews, which can help to motivate workers, rather than be set up and forgotten about.

Tania's performance improvement plan should be based on evidence of an irrefutable performance gap. Then, although other factors may need to be taken into account, you should have persuaded Tania of her responsibility for the problem. Then improvement can be planned.

A plan that prioritizes actions against company objectives is best, and one that produces some form of immediate result is motivating. The plan is most effective when the timetable for it is jointly set and includes periodic reviews.

Performance improvement plans won't naturally be evident. They have to be crafted and managed to be effective. This topic has shown you how to craft such a plan.

The reasons to use an employee assistance program

The reasons to use an employee assistance program

Performance problems are usually related to work, but sometimes problems are caused by other issues in the worker's life. You must establish the best way to handle this sort of problem.

Earl's performance at work has deteriorated lately, so his manager, Joyce, calls him into her office for a talk.

Joyce: Earl, I wanted to talk to you about your work. I've noticed that you haven't been as active as usual. Your sales are down by about 30 percent this month. Can you explain?

Earl: Well, not really.

Joyce: Come on, Earl. You're not making any sales. I want to know why.

Problem Performance Management

Earl: Things have been a bit difficult for me, but I've got everything under control now. I'll soon be selling as well as ever.

Joyce: Earl, we've known each other for years. What's up?

Earl: Joyce, I don't want to talk to you about this. I'm having some marital difficulties. Joyce: Oh, I see.

Joyce is right to be concerned about Earl's poor performance, and she is right to question him about it. But now she is faced with an issue that is best handled by experts from outside the organization. If he agrees, she should refer him to an employee assistance program. Employee assistance programs are purchased from other companies. They offer professional counselors who will provide confidential assessment and short-term counseling to employees and their families.

Of course, personal problems cannot be absolutely defined, but employee assistance programs generally deal with a variety of problems, such as:

- health
- marriage and family life
- drugs, including alcohol
- legal matters
- stress.

The reasons for using an employee assistance program can be related to the three elements of the working situation.

Employees

Employees are offered a professional service to themselves and their families at no cost. Counseling, and other supportive approaches, enable employees to continue earning. Confidentiality ensures that workers can seek assistance without detriment to their careers.

Managers

These programs allow managers to refer personal problems to professional counselors. So managers do not have to attempt to offer such a service when they are not trained to do so. They are also absolved from trying to deal with the confidentiality issues that would compromise their roles.

Employers

Statistics show that dollar for dollar, these programs save employers money. Absenteeism, and reduced turnover figures, suggest that the return on investment can be as much as sixteen-fold. Some studies also suggest that productivity can be significantly increased by such programs.

As well as financial benefits to companies, there are less tangible reasons for using employee assistance programs.

Employees

Jean was worried that her drug problem would lead to dismissal. But she was convinced of the confidentiality of the program's counselors. They helped her to stop using drugs, and now she has been promoted.

Managers

In Dan's previous company, an employee told him about her depression. Dan asked HR for help, and the employee was dismissed. Dan knows that an assistance program will prevent him from being placed in such a position again.

Employers

Digicom Inc. introduced a program for financial reasons. But the grateful letters from families supported by the program showed that the company had gained a lot of employee loyalty and goodwill in the community as well.

Question

Joel has been asked to make a presentation to three groups in the company about the reasons for establishing an employee assistance program. Help Joel match each group to one or more corresponding reasons for establishing the program.

Options:

A. employees
B. managers
C. employers

Targets:

1. do not have to offer a service they are not trained to do
2. will gain from professional service at no cost
3. can achieve sixteen-fold return on investment
4. can seek assistance without detriment to their career
5. will gain from reduced turnover figures

Answer

In fact, employees gain by receiving professional advice without affecting their careers. Employers will see a return on investment and reduce staff turnover, and managers won't be asked to offer a service that they aren't trained to give.

These programs allow managers to refer personal problems to professional counselors. Managers are also absolved from trying to deal with the confidentiality issues that would compromise their roles.

Counseling, and other supportive approaches, enable employees to continue earning and incur no out-of-pocket expenses for them.

Statistics show that dollar for dollar, these programs save employers money. This is due to reduced absenteeism and reduced turnover. Some studies also suggest that such programs can increase productivity.

Because of the total confidentiality of the counselors in an employee assistance program, employees do not have to worry about any negative effect on their work situation.

An employee assistance program enables employees with performance problems to become productive, contributing employees. Such employees can be retained instead of replaced, reducing employee turnover.

Employee assistance programs have definite benefits. According to a research paper published by Fisher Vista, an HR marketing company, 88 percent of Fortune 500 companies offer an employee assistance program.

Section 2 - Supporting Improvement

Problem performers cost money. Here are some examples:
- lack of productivity costs,
- replacement costs,
- support costs.

You can determine a general estimate of these costs. For example, say you have 50 employees, and average annual earnings per employee are $35,000. Now you have some idea of the relative costs of problem performers.

Training is one of the most common, and perhaps misused, responses to problem performance in the workplace. For many managers, it's a knee-jerk reaction that is often poorly designed and ineffective.

Training effectiveness is often considered purely in terms of the actual training event. In fact, effectiveness is a product of the stages that lead up to, and then spin off from, the training session.

Sports coaching has produced many famous quotations. The following quote, attributed to Ara Parseghian, epitomizes the importance of effective coaching on workplace performance:

"A good coach will make his players see what they can be, rather than what they are." To make coaching effective, the coach has to possess some important qualities. Select each of the characters to find out how they approach the process of coaching their teams. Determine your impression of them as coaches.

To ensure that the conduct of managers and supervisors in supporting workers has the maximum impact on improving performance, it must be tightly controlled.

The way managers and supervisors react to problem performance directly affects the likelihood of that performance occurring again.

Supporting improvement in workplace performance

Problem performers cost money. Here are some examples:
- • lack of productivity costs
- • replacement costs
- • support costs

You can determine a general estimate of these costs. For example, say you have 50 employees, and average annual earnings per employee are $35,000. Now you have some idea of the relative costs of problem performers.

Lack of productivity

A conservative estimate suggests that around 5 percent of the workforce can be considered problem performers. If you then assume that their productivity is around 50 percent of what it should be, lack of productivity will cost you approximately $45,000 per year.

Replacement costs

Assume that you are forced to replace two workers each year because of problem performance. Replacement costs are around 200 percent of salary. Performance will be limited, say 80 percent, for the first six months as the new workers learn the job. This adds up to $168,000.

Support costs

It has been shown that companies spend an average of 2 percent of payroll costs on training. So for this example, this would amount to $35,000 per year.

These sums suggest that problem performance costs this company approximately $213,000 per year, and training support costs $35,000. Even substantial increases in your training budget are justified by the cost of problem performance.

The comparative advantage of developing improved performance through support and training is immense. And spending money on support will, of course, reduce the other costs.

So the benefits of supporting improvement in workplace performance are:
- • limited comparative cost to your company,
- • reduced productivity losses,
- • reduced expenditure on replacing problem performers.

Turner, the head of human resources at Cellfast, explains the quantifiable benefits of supporting improvement to Cathy, an external HR consultant.

Turner: For me, the best example is one of our technical guys. He's extremely important to us because he builds and monitors all of our test rigs. So when his performance declined, we were really concerned. He was struggling to build new equipment to test to higher tolerances.

Cathy: Nobody is irreplaceable.

Turner: I know, but the costs of replacing this guy's expertise were staggering. We knew that if we could support him through the problem period and get him back on track, then we'd be so much better off. So we sent him to a refresher course at MIT.

Cathy: I bet that wasn't cheap!

Turner: You're right, but even so, it didn't come close to the cost of rebuilding the rigs and repeating the tests. Add that to the cost of recruiting a new technician, and we could have tripled the costs of the course--and still come out ahead.

Question

Denise has to justify training expenses to support problem performers in her workplace. What are the benefits of supporting performance improvement?

Options:

1. It will reduce productivity losses linked to problem performance.

2. It will ensure effective working relationships.

3. It will be of limited comparative cost.

4. It will reduce the expenditure on replacing problem performers.

5. It will decrease the cost of supervision.

Answer

Denise's organization will benefit from supporting performance improvement because it costs comparatively little, and reduces productivity losses and replacement costs for workers.

Option 1: Correct. It is estimated that around 5% of the workforce are problem performers. If they are 50% productive, the company is losing money on their lack of productivity. Improving their productivity will save money.

Option 2: Incorrect. Performance improvement is directed at improving worker productivity, not workplace relationships.

Option 3: Correct. The support cost is much less than the costs of replacement or the costs of low worker productivity.

Option 4: Correct. Replacement costs are high. Performance improvement will allow a company to retain more employees by supporting them until they are more productive, instead of replacing them.

Option 5: Incorrect. Performance improvement does not replace the role of supervisors.

Supporting improvement in the workplace makes sound economic sense. If you have an eye on the bottom line, you must take this approach before considering more drastic responses.

Training techniques to improve problem performance

Training techniques to improve problem performance

Training is one of the most common, and perhaps misused, responses to problem performance in the workplace. For many managers, it's a knee-jerk reaction that is often poorly designed and ineffective.

Training effectiveness is often considered purely in terms of the actual training event. In fact, effectiveness is a product of the stages that lead up to, and then spin off from, the training session.

Analysis

You need to identify the performance gaps that training can help improve. This usually consists of three forms: knowledge, skills, and attitudes. Often this aspect is referred to as a training needs analysis (TNA).

Design

You must consider the methods of, and approach to, the training intervention. There are a variety of training methods. You need to consider which are the most appropriate to meet the identified training needs.

Evaluation

You must identify the impact of training. You need a measure that relates the situation before the training to the situation after the training. Quantifiable measures are best, but subjective assessments also have a place.

Beatrice, Evan and Mitch have created effective training programs that have improved performance in their companies.

Mitch

"Training here used to be so unfocused. It was just a 'good thing' that nobody questioned. But I introduced a simple Training Needs Analysis model. Now if managers want training, they must assess current performance and indicate exactly what they expect the training to achieve."

Beatrice

"Our training programs are carefully designed. Only elements related to the Training Needs Analysis are covered. And we emphasize that the training method must relate to the training need. It's pretty simple once you've determined which methods work best for knowledge, skill, or attitude improvements."

Evan

"We measure training effectiveness by the impact it has on performance. That means we measure performance before the training--and after. We use quantitative measures if we can. Otherwise, we use the manager's assessment."

Question

Problem Performance Management

Ralph was asked to determine the critical stages that the company needs to consider to make training effective in improving performance. Which points should he make?

Options:

1. We must measure the situation before, and after, the training.
2. The training must be based on a needs analysis.
3. We have to improve the marketing of the training so that we increase attendance.
4. We need to ensure that we use training methods appropriate to the performance gap.

Answer

In fact, effective training includes analysis, design, and evaluation stages.

Option 1: Correct. This is how you identify the impact of training. Quantifiable measures are best, but subjective assessments can also be useful.

Option 2: Correct. A training needs analysis identifies the performance gaps that training can help improve. This usually consists of three forms: knowledge, skills, and attitudes.

Option 3: Incorrect. Training marketing and attendance are not measures of the training's effectiveness.

Option 4: Correct. You need to identify both the performance gaps that training can help improve and the best methods of, and approach to, the training intervention.

The purpose of training is to improve performance. This fact can easily be forgotten because some organizations overemphasize the lead-in and follow-up stages. These stages should be rigorous, but practical--they shouldn't demand too much time and money.

Analysis

Establish what people need to know for the job--often academic knowledge is too much. Differentiate skills into cognitive, perceptual, and motor categories so that appropriate training responses can be made. Attitudes are very difficult to change.

Design

Use methods appropriate to the learning need. Methods to develop knowledge include lectures and reading. A physical skill is developed through real and practical tasks. Attitudes are most likely to be changed through simulations and role plays.

Evaluation

The impact of the training needs to be measured on the workers' knowledge, skills, or attitudes, and in the way they now perform. The first impact can be measured by immediate tests, but the second requires time to demonstrate itself.

Case Study: Question 1 of 3

Scenario

You have been asked to develop a training program for some assembly workers. Their performance is not meeting targets, and your investigation has revealed one of the problems: The workers are not using the spot welding machinery effectively.

Show how you would develop a training program to improve this performance by answering the questions in order.

Question

You start by conducting a training needs analysis. Which would be the most appropriate recommendations from this analysis?

Problem Performance Management

Options:
1. Spot welding is a motor skill.
2. The workers need a program that changes their attitudes about the job.
3. These workers need to take a course on thermodynamic engineering.
4. They need a refresher course on how to use the spot welding equipment.

Answer

In fact, you need to identify what the workers need to know to do the job, and establish the skill that is required for improved performance.

Option 1: Correct. You must establish what people need to know for the job. Decide if the skill fits in the cognitive, perceptual, or motor category.

Option 2: Incorrect. Analysis includes deciding what type of skill is needed for the job. In this case, the needed skill is a motor skill and does not include a need for an attitude change.

Option 3: Incorrect. Thermodynamic engineering is a cognitive skill that is not required for this job.

Option 4: Correct. You have identified the exact skill that is needed, and which course of action to recommend.

Case Study: Question 2 of 3

You need to design an appropriate training program to improve their spot welding. Which statement best describes an appropriate program?

Options:
1. Improving the skill of spot welding requires a course with lots of physical, practical tasks.
2. Improving the skill of spot welding requires a course with plenty of reading about different welding systems.

3. Improving the skill of spot welding requires a course that uses plenty of role plays.

Answer

Actually, a skill is best taught by a course that includes plenty of practical tasks.

Option 1: Correct. A motor skill is developed through real and practical physical tasks.

Option 2: Incorrect. Reading is one way of improving a knowledge skill. Spot welding requires a training program that will improve a motor skill.

Option 3: Incorrect. Role plays are an effective way to encourage a change in attitude. Improving a motor skill needs a training program that includes physical tasks.

Case Study: Question 3 of 3

You want to identify whether the training program you have designed has been effective. Which examples describe your approach?

Options:

1. a test at the beginning and end of the training course to see whether spot welding skills have improved

2. an evaluation of the course by the welders

3. a review with their manager a few weeks later to see whether they have applied these new skills and improved their job performance

4. an immediate assessment by their manager of the change in their overall performance

Answer

In fact, a before and after assessment is required for an evaluation of skills. This can be performed at the end of the course. The evaluation of the impact on overall performance must occur when the skills have had time to be embedded.

Option 1: Correct. You must identify the impact of training. You need a measure that relates the situation before the training to the situation after the training.

Option 2: Incorrect. More objective evaluation measures such as quantitative measures and managers' assessments are a better approach.

Option 3: Correct. Quantitative measures are a very accurate way to record progress, but a manager's assessment can also be useful.

Option 4: Incorrect. An improvement in performance requires time to demonstrate itself. A managers' assessment that takes place a few weeks after training is a more accurate evaluation tool.

To ensure that training is effective, you need to conduct a training needs analysis that identifies the knowledge needed by workers, and differentiates the skill requirements. You then need to design a course that meets those needs. The skill of spot welding requires a practical, task-based course.

The program needs an appropriate evaluation to measure the skill before, and immediately after, the training. However, the impact of the training on the overall job performance cannot be properly assessed for some time.

Coaching methods to improve problem performance

Coaching methods to improve problem performance

Sports coaching has produced many famous quotations. The following quote, attributed to Ara Parseghian, epitomizes the importance of effective coaching on workplace performance:

"A good coach will make his players see what they can be, rather than what they are." To make coaching effective, the coach has to possess some important qualities. Select each of the characters to find out how they approach the process of coaching their teams. Determine your impression of them as coaches.

Colin

"While completing my master's degree, I performed research into the role of the salesperson in reducing customer defection. So I can explain to my team the theoretical models that underpin the paradigm of customer loyalty."

Gayle

"I work at an instinctive level. I show my team members how I do it, and then they know what to do. I find it difficult to explain how to tell the difference between the right way to fix things and the way that causes more problems."

Emily

"I emphasize effort. Everyone who tries hard enough can do this job well. The workers who just won't try get one chance with me. If they don't shape up, they're out."

Bobbie

"I remember when I had to learn how to do their job. You have to learn so much. I start them off with something simple and build their confidence. Then they can develop their own style, and do the background reading as they need it."

Colin is an expert in his field. But expertise may make the task more complicated than it needs to be. Gayle, on the other hand, can't explain the task. It's all in her head, and she finds it impossible to break it down. Emily is just as competent as Gayle, but she doesn't have the patience to work with people who struggle to perform. For her, the task is easy, so she always equates poor performance with laziness.

Bobbie has a different approach to coaching. She has a thorough grounding in the task, but she doesn't need to impress people with it. She is good at explaining how to do it and has the patience to work with learners and people who struggle to perform. Bobbie has all the qualities of an effective coach.

Sufficient expertise

She knows how to do the task properly, and she can recognize a variety of ways to achieve effective performance.

Teaching skills

She can show someone how to do the task. This is a different skill from just being able to do it yourself.

A supportive approach

She understands that not everyone will pick up the task quickly--but self-confidence is invariably the key to better performance.

Question

Leon is trying to decide whom to ask to take on the role of coaching the sales team. Which statements will help him to choose a suitable coach?

Options:

1. A coach must have an understanding of the psychology of the problem performer.

2. A coach must not demand too much.

3. A coach must have enough expertise, but not be overbearing.

4. A coach must know how to teach the skills needed to perform the task.

5. A coach must perceive the role as supporting problem performers. 6. A coach must not explain too much.

Answer

Actually, the qualities of an effective coach are sufficient expertise and teaching skills, and a supportive attitude.

Option 1: Incorrect. This is not a necessary skill for a coach to have. They need to support problem performers, but they do not need to understand them.

Option 2: Incorrect. Coaches need to be able to modify the task so that they can teach it to everyone, but they should not limit their expectations.

Option 3: Correct. A successful coach should know how to do the task properly, and recognize a variety of ways to achieve effective performance.

Option 4: Correct. A successful coach needs to be able to show someone how to do the task; a different skill from having mastered completion of the task.

Option 5: Correct. A good coach understands that not everyone will pick up the task quickly; they are willing and able to provide the support to build the confidence gradually. Confidence is the key to better performance.

Option 6: Incorrect. A coach needs to adapt the task or problem to the learning style and ability of each individual learner. The amount of explaining done will be different for each student.

Effective coaching requires expertise, teaching skills, and a supportive attitude. So how do you coach the coaches to ensure that these qualities are evident in the way that they operate?

Expertise

Avoid jargon--it can demotivate. Knowledge should be used to explain, not mystify. Use expertise to put the task into a context so that workers can see the whole job, not just disconnected parts.

Teaching

Prepare the instruction in a sensible, sequential order. Break the whole task down into digestible chunks. Link the training, wherever possible, to the existing experience and knowledge of the worker.

Support

The best approach is to show and explain, and then allow the workers to practice the skill. People learn by making mistakes, so this is a time to give encouragement. Continue to give motivational feedback throughout the performance.

Elroy is Yvonne's manager. Yvonne has recently transferred onto Elroy's team from another department in the organization, and she didn't have access to a computer in her previous role.

Now, although Elroy arranged for her to attend a short training course introducing her to the basics of computing, she still has problems using e-mail attachments.

Elroy decides that he needs to take some time out to coach Yvonne. He arranges to meet her in his office and begins by explaining that he would like her to learn how to attach documents to e-mail messages.

Yvonne: What's the point? I can put all the information in the body of the message.

Elroy: When you start sending the annual reports, you will need to send large documents in a variety of formats. It would be very time consuming and difficult to send them out in the main message. And attachments save time because they allow you to transfer existing documents without rewriting them.

Yvonne: Well, OK. But how do I do it?

Elroy: You'll usually attach spreadsheets, text documents, and images. But occasionally you'll have to send a database, which means you'll have to check which application it was written in, and which application the receiver has available.

Yvonne: Oh. I'm not sure I really understand.

Problem Performance Management

Elroy: OK. Why don't you watch me do it? Then maybe you can practice sending some e-mails with attachments to me.

Elroy did a fair job of coaching Yvonne--but he could have done better. He started well by using his expertise to put the task of adding attachments into the context of Yvonne's job. He also used his knowledge to explain the task to Yvonne without confusing her. However, when Elroy started to teach Yvonne how to attach a document, he baffled Yvonne with jargon and unnecessary information. He should have broken the task down into digestible chunks, and then linked it to what Yvonne already knew.

In the end, Elroy supported Yvonne well. By showing Yvonne how to do the task, and by encouraging her to practice and to make mistakes, Elroy did a great job of providing support for Yvonne during the learning process.

Throughout the coaching, you should have been supportive of John, and you should have shown him the techniques you advocate. He needs support while trying these new techniques, and encouragement when he makes mistakes.

Developing yourself and others to be effective coaches is a productive and efficient way of improving the performance of your workforce.

Using management and supervision techniques

Using management and supervision techniques

To ensure that the conduct of managers and supervisors in supporting workers has the maximum impact on improving performance, it must be tightly controlled.

The way managers and supervisors react to problem performance directly affects the likelihood of that performance occurring again.

This statement is based on the psychological model of behaviorism, which proposes that performance is influenced by the actions leading up to it, and the responses of significant people to the performance.

Operant conditioning is an aspect of behaviorist theory developed by B.F. Skinner. The theory is based on three elements:
- • antecedents,
- • behavior,

- • consequences.

Supervisors prompt performance through policies, targets, and so on. But the way that they respond to the performance, whether good or bad, is a supervisor's most powerful tool. This is the consequences stage of the operant conditioning model. Consequences are based on the idea of reinforcement. When supervisors praise a worker, they are reinforcing the performance. But reinforcement comes in various forms, resulting in different consequences.

Positive reinforcement

Positive reinforcement increases the possibility that the poor performance will occur more frequently in the future. Praise is a common reinforcer, but any attention may also do this. So be careful that you positively reinforce the behavior that you want.

Negative reinforcement

Negative reinforcement--although it may not sound like it--strengthens a behavior because a negative condition is stopped, or avoided, as a consequence of the behavior. So workers will repeat their good performances to avoid being reprimanded.

Punishment

Punishment weakens a behavior because a negative condition is introduced or experienced as a consequence of the behavior. So in this case, workers will not perform in a certain way because if they do, they will be reprimanded.

Extinction

In the extinction stage, a particular behavior is weakened by the consequence of not experiencing a positive condition, or stopping a negative condition. So workers stop a certain behavior--good or bad--because no one pays it any attention.

So when these different consequences are applied by supervisors and managers, how do they affect the performance of the workers?

Dawn

Dawn usually left her team members alone, but when they joked and fooled around in the office, she always told them to get back to work. Then she continued to talk to them. The jokes increased. Her attention reinforced the behavior.

Cliff

Cliff expected his team members to always wear their safety hats. If they did, he praised them, but if they didn't, he loudly reprimanded them. The workers didn't like to hear Cliff shout, so he negatively reinforced the wearing of hard hats.

Val

Val had an intolerant attitude to any workers who were late. She insisted that they replace, and double, any lost time at the normal end of the working day. This punishment ensured that most of the workers tried very hard not to be late.

Astrid

Astrid knew that Bill, one of her team members, had worked late on his own initiative to complete a vital task. She didn't mention it. The next time Bill needed to stay late, he didn't. Astrid had extinguished that behavior by not paying attention to it.

So remember that reinforcement doesn't always work in obvious ways. Dawn thought that telling her staff to get back to work would stop their behavior. But because they wanted her attention, and they only received it when they joked about, they increased that behavior. Cliff, on the other hand, provided both positive and negative reinforcement, so his team members responded to his reprimands in the way that he wanted.

Although Val thought she was getting her staff members to be on time, in fact, all she was doing was making sure that they didn't come in late! And Astrid's failure to respond in any way to Bill meant that there were no consequences to that behavior, so he stopped doing it.

Question

Harry wants to make sure that he correctly reinforces the behavior of his team members. Help Harry by matching each of the four aspects of reinforcement to the appropriate statement.

Options:

A. positive reinforcement
B. negative reinforcement
C. punishment
D. extinction

Targets:

1. Behavior will be strengthened to avoid this consequence.

2. Behavior is weakened by inattention.

3. This increases the possibility that the poor performance will occur more frequently.

4. Behavior will be weakened to avoid this consequence.

Answer

Positive reinforcement increases the chance that the issue will recur, whereas negative reinforcement causes an improvement to avoid consequences. Behavior will weaken to avoid punishment and extinction weakens through inattention.

Negative reinforcement strengthens a behavior because a negative condition is stopped, or avoided, as a consequence of the behavior.

In the extinction stage, a particular behavior is weakened by a lack of consequence. Workers stop a certain behavior--good or bad--because no one pays it any attention.

Positive reinforcement increases the possibility that the poor performance will occur more frequently in the future. Praise is a common reinforcer, but any attention may also do this.

Punishment weakens a behavior because a negative condition is introduced or experienced as a consequence of the behavior.

There are numerous ways to reinforce positive performance, but whatever approach you take, there are certain golden rules about the use of reinforcers.

Personalized

You must use reinforcers that fit with your personal management style. You must give the reinforcement in a personal way. Calling someone by his or her name or nickname is a simple way to achieve this.

Sincerity

You must express the reinforcement message sincerely. Any humor or dishonesty will devalue the process. You cannot approach reinforcement as a ritual or routine process. Each reinforcement must be genuine.

Specificity

The receivers of the reinforcement must understand why they are receiving them. You must clearly describe the behavior you are reinforcing so that there are no doubts.

Immediacy

The reinforcer must be given as close to the behavior as possible, preferably while workers are performing the act. The greater the gap between behavior and reinforcement, the less impact there will be on subsequent behavior.

Now you can see that the way you praise or reprimand your workers is vital to the development of good performance.

Section 3 - Changing the Work Situation
Section 3 - Changing the Work Situation

Performance problems are often thought to be the responsibility of the individual workers, but this isn't always true. Performance problems can also stem from:
- the way the job is organized,
- the impact of working on a team on individual performance,
- the management practices that are chosen to improve performance.

One effective way to improve workplace performance is to focus on the design and structure of the task that you are asking your workers to perform. Most workers are performing as members of a team, and their performances can be affected by that membership.

Working in teams can be tremendously beneficial. Collective problem-solving can be more effective than the ideas of one individual, and by pooling expertise, teams can be remarkably productive. But teams can also affect individual performance negatively.

The management practices an organization adopts will have an impact on performance improvement, but organizations come in many forms. So can you adapt

Problem Performance Management

management actions to improve performance to fit the organization?

Changing the work situation

Changing the work situation

Performance problems are often thought to be the responsibility of the individual workers, but this isn't always true. Performance problems can also stem from:

- the way the job is organized,
- the impact of working on a team on individual performance,
- the management practices that are chosen to improve performance.

Explore the causes of problem performance as described by Tony, Geraldine, and Alana.

Tony: The trouble with this place is that the managers think we're only here for the money. But the job's so boring, no one can stand it for long. I really think that if the bosses tried to improve job satisfaction, then performance would improve. But the managers keep talking about how good the productivity bonuses are.

Problem Performance Management

Geraldine: I'm part of a team of more than 30 workers. Communication is poor, and when you rely on other people in the team, productivity suffers. I've suggested that we form some smaller teams, but no one seems to see any relationship between team size and performance.

Alana: We're supposed to be high achievers and self-starters. But I think that's just an excuse to avoid spending the company's time and effort on developing our skills. We're supposed to do that on our own time. Well, people lose enthusiasm for that pretty quickly. So high performance starts to taper off.

The common thread running through these examples is the failure of the organization to change the work situation to improve performance. If the organization did change the work situation, then it would:

- avoid inappropriate individual blame,
- reinforce team synergies,
- adopt collective, cost-effective performance improvement measures.

Some organizations are reluctant to admit that they, not the individual workers, are to blame for some aspects of problem performance. When these organizations admit responsibility, they are on the way to recovery.

Question

Leon has repeatedly told his colleagues that performance improvement also requires the company to change the work situation. What benefits of changing the work situation should he cite?

Options:

1. "By changing the work situation, we don't have to admit that we are responsible for some elements of problem performance."
2. "Changing the work situation will help us avoid inappropriately blaming individual workers for performance problems."
3. "One benefit of changing the work situation is that we can adopt collective, cost-effective performance improvement measures."
4. "We can reinforce team synergies by changing the team working situation."
5. "Changing the work situation will mean that we can consider poor management to be responsible for some performance problems."

Answer

In fact, the benefits of changing the work situation are that it helps you avoid blaming individual workers, team synergies are revitalized, and performance improvement is collective and cost-effective.

Option 1: Incorrect. It is important to place the blame where it rightfully belongs. Otherwise, Leon's company will be unable to implement effective measures to improve the situation.

Option 2: Correct. Taking this attitude concerning the situation will help Leon's company to correctly place blame, and identify corrective measures.

Option 3: Correct. By adopting such measures, Leon's company will be improving the workplace by providing positive motivators for employees to perform well.

Option 4: Correct. When the team situation supports, rather than detracts, from the team synergies, the employees will be more satisfied with their working environment.

Option 5: Incorrect. Changing the work situation is about making improvements, not about assuming blame.

Changing the work situation provides you with cost-effective, fair, and productive responses to performance problems.

Changing the design of the task to improve performance

Changing the design of the task to improve performance

One effective way to improve workplace performance is to focus on the design and structure of the task that you are asking your workers to perform.

If you suspect that the task is not optimized for performance, then you need to isolate some of the factors in the task design that are most likely to affect productivity.

Interest

An interesting job provides intrinsic motivational factors, such as challenge and pride; a less interesting job relies more on extrinsic factors, such as pay and bonus rates. Intrinsic motivation is more powerful and long-lasting than extrinsic motivation.

Sequence

Problem Performance Management

The way a task relates to another task has a potential impact on performance. If task A has to wait for task B, then performance could be affected. Inefficient flow and sequence within a task could hinder performance.

Ergonomics

The design of workstations, tools, equipment, layouts, and processes affects performance. You should optimize the capabilities of employees by removing any obvious barriers to productivity and performance.

In many organizations, the design of the task is taken for granted. The way the task was constructed may have been based on arbitrary or outdated principles. The end result is a task designed not to optimize performance but to limit it. Claire, Phil, and Geoff work in organizations where this is the case.

Claire

"Nobody values what I do. I know the salespeople are the stars, but nothing would work here if I didn't arrange the delivery of the goods they sell. All I get is criticism when things don't arrive on time. They don't really care what I do, and I'm afraid that, lately, neither do I."

Phil

"Rob is supposed to check the customer's credit rating before he forwards the information on to me. I enter the customer details in the system, which takes forever. Three times last week, I entered data, and then Rob told me that the customers' credit had been declined. This job is pointless."

Geoff

"I tell you, working here is no fun. I process the invoices as they arrive. But I've got to collect them from all over the place. My desk is in the warehouse--it's so noisy, I can't concentrate. I used to sort the invoices at home, but now I think, 'Why should I?'"

Question

Ramon's team members have performance problems, which he suspects are based on the inefficient and ineffective design of the tasks that the workers are expected to do. Which statements identify the factors that support his view?

Options:

1. To get supplies, the packing supervisor has to get the key from the warehouse supervisor--if she can find him.

2. The packer's job is repetitive and boring. None of them are expected to take any pride in their work.

3. The packers always work too quickly so that they get the bonus rate.

4. Because they don't think it's their job, the administrators date-stamp orders last, leaving the packers insufficient time to complete the orders within the day.

5. The day shift packers are in a dispute with the night shift packers over work station cleanliness.

Answer

Actually, performance is affected by job interest, job sequence, and ergonomics.

Option 1: Correct. The way a task relates to another task has a potential impact on performance. In this case, performance is affected by the fact that the packing supervisor has to get the key from the supervisor.

Option 2: Correct. An interesting job provides intrinsic motivational factors, such as challenge and pride; a less interesting job, such as the packer's job, relies more on extrinsic factors, such as pay and bonus rates.

Option 3: Incorrect. The factors that contribute to performance problems based on inefficient and ineffective task design are job interest, job sequence, and ergonomics. This situation is not related to one of these.

Option 4: Correct. The design of processes is one of several factors that affect performance. Ramon's company should optimize the capabilities of employees by removing any obvious barriers to productivity and performance.

Option 5: Incorrect. This situation is not related to one of the three factors that contribute to performance problems caused by insufficient task design. The three factors are job interest, job sequence, and ergonomics.

How do you change the design and structure of the task so that you are optimizing performance?

Interest

Increase intrinsic motivation by making the work more valued by the company. Employees have to be empowered to take more responsibility for problem-solving and target-setting. If possible, the scope of the job should be enriched.

Sequence

Observe and evaluate the sequence and interdependency of tasks. Then redesign the work to optimize performance, with explicit targets in the case of dependent tasks. Introduce an agreed-upon task sequence that follows the most effective work flow.

Ergonomics

Fit the task, process, and work situation to the individual, not the other way around. Arrange tools for optimum use. Consider cognitive ergonomics, in which factors in the environment that hinder thinking and concentration are eliminated.

Case Study: Question 1 of 3
Scenario

Ruth is an administrative assistant in the sales department. You are her supervisor, and you have some concerns that Ruth is not performing to her maximum. You feel that Ruth really seems to try hard, but the structure and design of her job may be at fault.

Demonstrate how you could improve Ruth's performance by answering the questions in order.

Question

Ruth is responsible for the preferred customer records. Preferred customers are the big, regular spenders, and Ruth sends them information about new products and invites them to discount nights at the stores around the state. Ruth sees this as a mundane and uninteresting task. How could you improve her performance?

Options:

1. I'd widen the scope of Ruth's job by involving her in the organization of the discount nights in the stores.

2. I'd tell her that if she doesn't change her attitude, I'll give that task to someone who will be more enthusiastic about it.

3. I'd encourage Ruth to build a more detailed profile on each customer so that we can better target customers for new product launches.

4. I'd increase my supervision of Ruth to make sure that she wasn't underperforming.

Answer

In fact, Ruth's performance will improve if the scope of her job can be increased, and she is empowered more.

Option 1: Correct. You will increase Ruth's intrinsic motivation by making her work more valued to the company in this way.

Option 2: Incorrect. Threats are not a good way to improve an employee's motivation to do a good job. It would be preferable to widen the scope of her responsibilities and make her feel more valued in the company.

Option 3: Correct. By taking this action, you will be enriching the scope of Ruth's job. As a result, she will feel more valued, and her intrinsic motivation will increase.

Option 4: Incorrect. In order to improve Ruth's performance, you would do well to help her feel more valued by the company and, if possible, widen or enrich the scope of her job.

Case Study: Question 2 of 3

Ruth gets customer information from the sales team members when they remember to inform her. She frequently wastes time on customers who are no longer buying in sufficient quantity to be rated as preferred, or have changed their brands of merchandise. She sometimes isn't even informed about new preferred customers. How would you change this to improve performance?

Options:

1. Ruth should check with the sales team before she sends mailings to customers to ensure they are appropriate.

2. The sales team needs to be reminded of its responsibilities to Ruth.

3. The sales team members should be told that informing Ruth of new customers will be part of their performance appraisal.

4. Ruth should send the sales team members a copy of the mailings she has already sent to customers.

Then they can tell her whether the mailing was appropriate for those customers.

Answer

Actually, Ruth's performance will be improved by creating an effective work flow, and by setting targets for the sales force to ensure that its performance does not limit Ruth's.

Option 1: Correct. You can observe and evaluate the sequence and interdependency of Ruth's tasks and redesign the process in this way. This will increase her ability to perform her work effectively.

Option 2: Incorrect. This is a problem that is caused by sequencing issues. The way to address the problem is by observing the process and redesigning it to improve the workflow.

Option 3: Correct. This action can be the result of the redesign of this process that you performed after observing the workflow. This should have an impact on Ruth's ability to perform well.

Option 4: Incorrect. The object of redesigning the process is to improve the workflow. Redesigning the process in this way doesn't improve the workflow for Ruth.

Case Study: Question 3 of 3

Ruth shares a busy office with the three staff members who deal with complaints. Ruth only works each morning; this means that she relies on her colleagues to take messages for her. The sales team members usually call in the morning because they are traveling in the afternoons. What would you do in these circumstances to improve Ruth's performance?

Options:

1. I'd insist that Ruth starts working on afternoons.

2. I'd get voice mail for Ruth, and suggest to the sales team members that they try calling in the afternoon.

3. Ruth needs to be relocated to an environment that enables her to concentrate better.

4. I'd instruct Ruth's colleagues to tell her callers to call back when she is at work.

Answer

In fact, Ruth's performance will be improved by cognitive ergonomics, and by fitting the job to her--not the other way around.

Option 1: Incorrect. Ruth is likely to view this action as a punishment. It would be more effective to fit the job to meet her needs, rather than change her situation to fit the needs of the job.

Option 2: Correct. This issue is an ergonomics issue. By restructuring the job to fit Ruth's needs in this way, you will be enabling her to improve her performance.

Option 3: Correct. By doing this, you are improving the cognitive ergonomics for Ruth. Her mental ability to perform well will be increased.

Option 4: Incorrect. This option does not address the cognitive ergonomics that Ruth deals with. You should redesign the job to be centered on her needs and improve the cognitive ergonomics.

Ruth's performance can be improved if the scope of her job is increased by involving her in the organization of the discount nights in the stores, and by empowering her to build a more detailed profile on each customer. She can be helped by creating an effective flow to her work, and by setting targets for the sales force to ensure that its performance does not negatively affect hers. The way the job is fitted around her, rather than the other way around, will also help performance, as will consideration of cognitive ergonomics.

By changing the task, you can definitely improve performance with some simple adjustments. So increase the interest in the job, ensure that the job follows a sensible sequence, and adjust it to fit with ergonomic principles.

Managing team characteristics

Managing team characteristics

Most workers are performing as members of a team, and their performances can be affected by that membership.

Working in teams can be tremendously beneficial. Collective problem-solving can be more effective than the ideas of one individual, and by pooling expertise, teams can be remarkably productive. But teams can also affect individual performance negatively.

Size

The number of participants will affect performance. Decision-making and communication are affected by team size. Social loafing--not contributing on the assumption that someone else will perform--increases with increased team size.

Cohesiveness

Cohesiveness--the degree to which members are attracted to each other--affects individual performance. A cohesive group can have an attitude toward performance that will encourage, or discourage, individual productivity.

Social facilitation

Social facilitation is characterized by the way that performing a task in front of others can have both a positive and negative effect on performance. Some people are born performers, but others will hate the spotlight.

Brad, Eric, Tonya, and Helen are managers. Working in teams has affected individual performance in their organizations. Brad has experienced the positive effects of working in teams, but the others have not.

Brad

"We operated as a group of individual designers until our new CEO advocated more team work. The first time we worked together on a design, there were a few initial concerns, but the way we bounced ideas off each other was magic--and productive."

Eric

"The team became divided. The members argued constantly, even about simple things. I had a dozen team members accusing the rest of laziness, and refusing to work with them until they'd done their share."

Tonya

"When I took over the team, the members had been working together for more than five years. They were obviously coasting, and I told them they had to speed up. I could reason with them individually, but when they were all together, they just wouldn't listen."

Helen

"When the team members moved from individual offices to an open-plan layout, a couple of workers said that they just couldn't cope with everybody watching them. I really didn't believe them at first, but their productivity did seriously decline."

Question

Olive had been told that teamwork could have a negative effect on the performance of individual team members. What factors should she be concerned about?

Options:

1. The size of the team may affect individual performance.

2. Individual performance may be affected by team synergy.

3. Individual performance may be affected by team cohesiveness.

4. Pooled ideas in a team can negatively affect individual performance.

5. Some individuals may be adversely affected by having to perform their duties in front of other team members.

Answer

In fact, size, cohesiveness, and social facilitation can all have a negative impact on the individual performance of team members.

Option 1: Correct. Decision-making and communication are affected by team size. Also, social loafing-- not contributing on the assumption that someone else will perform--increases with increased team size.

Option 2: Incorrect. Individual team members' performance can be impacted by the team size, cohesiveness, and level of comfort in facilitation. The team's synergy is impacted by these factors, not the other way around.

Option 3: Correct. A cohesive group can have an attitude toward performance that will encourage, or discourage, individual productivity.

Option 4: Incorrect. Collective problem-solving can be more effective than the ideas of one individual, and by pooling expertise, teams can be remarkably productive.

Option 5: Correct. Performing a task in front of others can have both a positive and negative effect on performance. Some people are born performers, but others will hate the spotlight.

Managers must recognize the way that teamwork can affect individual performance and apply remedial actions to prevent or limit these effects.

Size

Consider the optimum size for your team. Between five and ten members will have the maximum benefit on communication, problem-solving, and decision-making. This size will limit social loafing. Larger teams are effective at fact-finding, smaller teams at action tasks.

Cohesiveness

Cohesiveness is positive when yoked with good attitudes to performance, so both need attention. Encourage cohesiveness by increasing the time the team members spend together, and stimulating competition with other teams. Encourage a good attitude by using collective rewards and praise.

Social facilitation

Simple routine tasks are improved by public performance, while complex work requiring more attention is not. Apply this in the work setting, and also in relation to training. Train for simple tasks in groups, and train for more complex tasks individually.

Case Study: Question 1 of 3
Scenario

You are the manager of a team of software designers. The team members have worked together well for the past two years. The team had been mainly concerned with identifying good designs, but more and more members are expected to produce their own designs, and some individuals are struggling. You decide to look at the way the team operates to try to improve individual performances.

Demonstrate how you will do this by answering the questions in order.

Question

The team consists of 13 designers, two senior designers, and four clerks. You ask a senior designer to evaluate the effectiveness of each individual. She reports that three designers and one clerk seem to be "loafing." Their work will require limited research but high levels of activity by all team members. How should you respond to this information?

Options:

1. I will split the team so that the social loafers cannot hide.

2. I'll leave them alone. I think the team is an optimum size.

3. I think that a smaller team would be more appropriate for taking actions, rather than fact-finding.

4. I think that the team is the ideal size now for activity-based tasks.

Answer

Actually, team size is optimally between five and ten members. The smaller teams will discourage social loafing and be more suited to activity than research.

Option 1: Correct. Between five and ten members will have the maximum benefit on communication, problem-solving, and decision-making. This size will limit social loafing.

Option 2: Incorrect. Social loafing increases with increased team size. Having between five and ten team members will limit it.

Option 3: Correct. Larger teams are effective at fact-finding, while smaller teams are more effective at action tasks.

Option 4: Incorrect. Smaller groups are more appropriate for activity-based tasks because it is easier to come to a resolution with fewer people. Larger groups are better at fact finding.

Case Study: Question 2 of 3

The team seems to have developed a negative attitude toward working overtime. You have approached some individuals who say that they would work overtime but do not want to upset their colleagues. Your boss recommends that you bring in new staff members and ensure that the team is less cohesive in the future. What should you do?

Options:

1. I would bring in new workers to diminish the cohesiveness of the team, and enable individuals to work to their potential.

2. I would not want to diminish cohesiveness--I'd tie it to a more positive attitude toward performance.

3. I'd encourage a more positive attitude toward performance by using rewards and praise.

4. I'd double the overtime rate to break the cohesiveness of the team by using extra rewards.

Answer

In fact, cohesiveness is a positive force on individual productivity when the team attitude is positive.

Option 1: Incorrect. Cohesiveness can be a good thing if it is focused on positive attitudes. Rather than destroying cohesiveness, you should try to improve it in a positive manner.

Option 2: Correct. Cohesiveness is positive when complimented with good attitudes to performance, so both need attention.

Option 3: Correct. You can encourage a good attitude by using collective rewards and praise, increasing the time the team members spend together, and stimulating competition with other teams.

Option 4: Incorrect. It is more effective to encourage cohesiveness in a positive way. You can use rewards to do this.

Case Study: Question 3 of 3

The team works in a large, open office. Team training events on software design are conducted in this office. The administrators have a small, separate cubicle where they can be individually trained in the straightforward record-filing system. How should you respond to this information?

Options:

1. The designers should get individual training on their more complex tasks.

2. The administrators can have group training for their simple tasks.

3. The software designers will work best in an open office where public attention will improve their performance.

4. The task of filing is likely to be improved by public attention.

Answer

In fact, public attention will not improve either the performance or training of complex tasks. But simple tasks will benefit from this approach.

Option 1: Correct. If you train for more complex tasks individually, people will generally feel more comfortable.

Option 2: Correct. Simple routine tasks are improved by public performance, while complex work requiring more attention is not.

Option 3: Incorrect. The software designers would be better served if their team training took place in the smaller area where they would be more likely to concentrate on the complex tasks.

Option 4: Correct. This is a simple, routine task and would be improved by the team's group effort, rather than an individual one.

Team size affects individual performance. The bigger teams are best at fact-finding tasks, while the smaller teams are more likely to perform well at activity-based tasks. Teams are most effective when membership is limited to around ten members.

Group cohesion is a positive force on individuals when allied with a good team attitude; otherwise it can be a negative force. And training for the performance of complex and simple tasks needs to be held in different settings.

Problem Performance Management

When you create a team, remember that the characteristics of that team need to be carefully controlled to enable maximum individual performance. And now you know how to do it!

Appropriate management practice

Appropriate management practice

The management practices an organization adopts will have an impact on performance improvement, but organizations come in many forms. So can you adapt management actions to improve performance to fit the organization?

One approach is to categorize organizations based on their performance levels, as defined by profitability, productivity, and quality. Organizations were classified as:

- • low performers
- • medium performers
- • high performers

The research, which was based on 580 companies in the auto, computer, banking, and health care industries in Japan, Germany, Canada, and the United States, matched 945 business practices with different levels of performance. The conclusions enable you to predict what type of management practice will improve performance in your type of organization.

Low performers
For low-performing organizations, the best approaches to managing improvement were organizing people into effective work teams and training. Self-managed and autonomous teams had little, or no, effect on performance.

Medium performers
Medium performers need to emphasize education and training. These companies also benefit when specific inputs are made to the workers about overall company performance assessments, and are related to their own performance.

High performers
High-performing companies benefit from benchmarking and employee empowerment approaches. But team-based approaches did not have any affect on performance. Continual training was not necessary to improve performance.

These companies have adopted appropriate management practices for each performance level.

Shackleton & Cooper
This low-performing company concentrated on improving performance on the factory floor. It has created a problem-solving team to improve the interaction between quality control and production. The team, made up of three representatives from each department, meets weekly.

Denillson Inc.
Denillson is a medium-performing organization. Its focus has been to ensure that the workforce is able to

adapt quickly to the new processes and equipment that the company has invested in. The company ensures that all workers are aware of its current market position.

Coatings International

As a high-performing organization, Coatings International has never been content to rest on its laurels. It benchmarks against its major competitors, and it is not afraid to learn the lessons from these comparisons, adapting its processes accordingly.

Question

Robbie recognizes that all organizations are not the same, but how can he differentiate between the management practices they should adopt to improve performance? Help him by matching each type of organization with one or more corresponding correct approaches.

Options:

A. low-performing organization
B. medium-performing organization
C. high-performing organization

Targets:

1. benefit from benchmarking
2. organize people into effective teams
3. autonomous teams have no effect on performance
4. emphasize education and training
5. ensure workers are aware of mission statements

Answer

In fact, low-performing organizations should ensure that their teams are effective; medium performers should ensure that the workers are educated and informed; high performers can use benchmarking techniques.

Problem Performance Management

High-performing companies benefit from benchmarking and employee empowerment approaches, and are not afraid to learn the lessons from these strategies, adapting its processes accordingly.

For low-performing organizations, the best approaches to managing improvement are organizing people into effective work teams and training. This increases the chances of improving the group's performance.

Self-managed and autonomous teams have little or no effect on performance. Managed, cross-functional teams are very beneficial in improving performance.

Medium performers will find the most benefit from emphasizing education and training. These companies also benefit when specific inputs are made to the workers about overall company performance assessments.

Robbie should strive to help the employees see the big picture in this way. Also, senior management participation at department-level meetings ensures that workers get information specific to their performance.

How can you apply these management practices to improve performance in the different types of organizations?

Low performers

Focus on developing effective work teams led by supervisors. Department-level meetings do not help performance much. Cross-functional teams are very beneficial, particularly those involving customers. Baseline training of all workers is essential.

Medium performers

Training should be based on understanding principles rather than programmed instruction. Senior management participation at department-level meetings ensures that workers get information specific to their performance.

High performers

High-performing organizations benchmark customer satisfaction measures and competitor comparison measures as part of their strategic planning cycles. Too many department-level team meetings limit empowerment.

Case Study: Question 1 of 3

Scenario

You are advising three companies--Turkeyland Inc., Consuela Realtors, and Abacta--as to the most effective management actions that would improve the performance of the workforces in their organizations.

Answer the questions in order.

Question

Turkeyland Inc. is a low-performing company. Which responses would indicate the appropriate actions that it should take to improve workplace performance?

Options:

1. The company should concentrate on the leadership function at the department level to improve worker performance.

2. Turkeyland must empower its workers to encourage them to improve their performance.

3. Effective baseline training of workers is absolutely necessary for Turkeyland to improve performance.

4. The company must benchmark itself against successful companies as the best way to work to achieve higher worker performance.

5. The company needs to develop a teamwork approach, concentrating on effective leadership by the supervisors.

Answer

In fact, for low-performing companies, the priority actions are ensuring baseline training, and the development of effective teams with good supervision.

Option 1: Incorrect. The best approaches to managing performance improvement in low-performing companies are organizing people into effective work teams and baseline training.

Option 2: Incorrect. Turkeyland would do well to provide baseline training for its employees. Also, the company should establish a team-based approach that concentrates of effective supervisor leadership.

Option 3: Correct. For low-performing organizations, one of the best approaches to managing improvement baseline training. This ensures that employees are up to date with the minimum amount required of them.

Option 4: Incorrect. This is a strategy for high-performing companies. Turkeyland would do better to focus on establishing a teamwork approach and providing baseline training.

Option 5: Correct. Low-performing organizations can manage improvement by organizing people into effective work teams that are properly managed, encouraging employees to better performance.

Case Study: Question 2 of 3

Consuela Realtors is a medium-performing company. What actions should it take to improve performance?

Options:

1. The company should concentrate on the principles behind procedures and skills by using a more theoretical approach to training and development.

2. The company would benefit from senior managers joining department-level meetings. The managers can inform the staff members about the current performance of the company.

3. Cross-functional teams would be a good idea to improve worker performance in this organization.

4. Consuela Realtors needs to benchmark itself against competitors. This would radically improve worker performance.

Answer

Actually, medium-performing companies need to focus on the department-level meetings, and a theoretical approach to training and development.

Option 1: Correct. Training should be based on understanding principles rather than programmed instruction. This helps employees to better understand how their job fits into the larger perspective.

Option 2: Correct. Senior management participation at department-level meetings ensures that workers get information specific to their performance. This allows employees to feel valued by senior management.

Option 3: Incorrect. This strategy is more appropriate for low-performing teams. Consuela Realtors will benefit more from concentrating on the principles behind procedures and skills, as well as getting senior manager input.

Option 4: Incorrect. This strategy is appropriate for high-performing companies. Consuela Realtors should focus on bringing the insights of senior managers to the employees, as well as concentrating on the principles behind procedures.

Case Study: Question 3 of 3

Abacta is a high-performing company. What recommendations would be appropriate for this company to improve the performance of its workers?

Options:

1. Companies like Abacta need to develop the baseline training of all of its workers.

2. Abacta should encourage good performance from its workers by empowering them.

3. This company should ensure that senior managers are very visible, and engaged at department-level meetings and briefings.

4. Abacta must benchmark against its major competitors to maintain the high performance of its employees.

Answer

In fact, high-performing companies need to concentrate on such activities as benchmarking, and empowerment of the workers.

Option 1: Incorrect. This is a strategy that most effectively works for low-performing companies. Abacta should focus its efforts on empowerment and benchmark comparisons.

Option 2: Correct. Too many department-level team meetings limit empowerment. By empowering the employees, Abacta will maximize its potential for raising employee performance.

Option 3: Incorrect. This is a great intervention for medium-performing companies, but Abacta is a high-performer and would be better served by focusing on benchmark comparisons and empowering its employees.

Option 4: Correct. High-performing organizations benchmark customer satisfaction measures and competitor comparison measures as part of their strategic planning cycles.

For low performers, such as Turkeyland Inc., the best approach to improving the performance of workers comes with baseline training and an effective team working approach. For Consuela Realtors, the medium-performing company, the theoretical aspects of its training methods should be promoted.

Medium companies need highly visible senior management involvement at department-level meetings. High performers, on the other hand, need to concentrate on empowering staff and using benchmarking techniques.

By determining what level of performance your company is achieving, you can identify the managerial actions that are most appropriate to improve worker performance in your organization.

CHAPTER 4 - Addressing Problem Performance

CHAPTER 4 - Addressing Problem Performance
 Section 1 - Disciplining Problem Performance
 Section 2 - The Conventional Progressive Disciplinary Approach
 Section 3 - Alternatives to the Conventional Approach to Discipline at Work

Section 1 - Disciplining Problem Performance

Section 1 - Disciplining Problem Performance

According to the Society for Human Resource Management, 60 percent of organizations have failed in at least one employment-related lawsuit, and have consequently paid a median award of $218,000. So, the consequences of the ineffective management of disciplinary proceedings can be punitive financially. But there are also human costs.

One of the biggest mistakes in management is inconsistent or unfair treatment of problem performers. The way to avoid this is to have an effective disciplinary policy. The disciplinary policy that a company uses should be a public document, and in fact, many organizations put a copy into employee handbooks. It should cover four main sections.

Effective discipline is always preceded by effective preparation. You must ensure that you are thorough and meticulous in preparing for any disciplinary proceeding that you have to carry out, if it is to be successful. Some managers, like Lester and Carol, have not heeded the lesson that effective preparation leads to effective disciplinary actions. And they have experienced negative results from this mistake.

Many employers think that because of the doctrine of employment-at-will, they can fire employees at any time, and for any reason. So discipline is easy. But those employers are wrong--some reasons for firing employees are illegal.

Employment-at-will is the major form of employment relationship, but employment contracts can be used to bind both employer and employee into a more controlled relationship. A contract is a deliberate act, but some employers find their actions limited by implied contracts. Also, the employment-at-will doctrine has other exceptions.

Disciplining problem performance effectively

According to the Society for Human Resource Management, 60 percent of organizations have failed in at least one employment-related lawsuit, and have consequently paid a median award of $218,000.

So, the consequences of the ineffective management of disciplinary proceedings can be punitive financially. But there are also human costs.

Dee: I decided to leave when the company failed to deal with Don's absenteeism again. He was just so blatant about taking sick leave whenever the horse races were in town. The company just kept on warning him, but didn't really do anything, while I had to work extra to cover his absence.

Dee says.

Problem Performance Management

Jack: I work with Don too, and if he can get away with being absent a lot without good reason, so can I. I can't wait for the fishing season!
Jack says.

Dee and Jack are just two employees affected by poorly organized discipline in their company. No doubt there will be many more. The benefits of disciplining problem performance effectively are:
- • avoiding punitive lawsuits
- • limiting employee turnover
- • maintaining good morale.

Effective disciplinary proceedings won't eliminate problem performance, but ineffective disciplinary proceedings will certainly increase it. Workers want fairness and consistency, not managers who make up the rules as they need them.

Question

In Jenny's company, disciplinary procedures were well handled and organized. Although she wasn't comfortable with disciplining employees, she could certainly see that there were definite benefits from disciplining problem performance effectively. Which statements support her view?

Options:

1. Effective disciplinary proceedings will maintain good morale among all employees.

2. When disciplinary proceedings are handled correctly, the company will avoid punitive lawsuits.

3. Effective discipline will put a stop to problem performance.

4. Good disciplinary proceedings are instrumental in limiting employee turnover.

5. Good disciplinary proceedings encourage flexibility in management.

Answer

In fact, the benefits of disciplining problem performance effectively lie in avoiding punitive lawsuits, limiting employee turnover, and maintaining good morale.

Option 1: Correct. When there is good morale, employees will feel positive about their work environment.

Option 2: Correct. Properly handled disciplinary meetings can decrease the potential of expensive lawsuits. Workers who feel that discipline is applied inconsistently may choose to sue.

Option 3: Incorrect. Each employee is still responsible for his or her own behavior, regardless of the quality of the disciplinary meeting.

Option 4: Correct. Employee turnover can be limited in various ways. Properly managed disciplinary meetings are one way to achieve this.

Option 5: Incorrect. While flexibility in management might be a desired management style, it isn't one of the benefits of properly run disciplinary proceedings.

Disciplining a worker is probably one of the hardest things a manager will do. So make sure you are going to get it right by completing this lesson.

Key features of an effective disciplinary policy

Key features of an effective disciplinary policy

One of the biggest mistakes in management is inconsistent or unfair treatment of problem performers. The way to avoid this is to have an effective disciplinary policy.

The disciplinary policy that a company uses should be a public document, and in fact, many organizations put a copy into employee handbooks. It should cover four main sections.

Principles

This section describes the reasons for, and purpose of, your disciplinary policy. In other words, what you are trying to achieve by it. It should clearly state what sorts of actions and behaviors are subject to the disciplinary policy.

Process

This section specifies how the disciplinary process works. It itemizes the usual steps in the procedure. It usually states that, under exceptional circumstances, you can eliminate certain steps.

Responses

This section explains what actions you might take, and the factors you might take into account in reaching your decision. Often it specifies, but does not limit itself to, the sorts of behaviors or actions that might result in automatic termination.

Provisos

This section might include any statements in relation to employment at will that allow you to act without recourse to the policy. It should cover any other deviations from policy that you might follow.

It's vital that any policy document is clear and unambiguous so that the obligations and rights of all concerned are clearly understood.

Question

Bill thought he knew what should be in his company's disciplinary policy. Help him by matching each section of the policy to one or more appropriate pieces of content.

Options:

A. Principles
B. process
C. responses
D. provisos

Targets:

1. itemize the usual steps in the procedure
2. statements in relation to employment at will
3. what you are trying to achieve by the policy

4. specify the sorts of behaviors or actions that might result in automatic termination

5. what sorts of actions and behaviors are subject to the disciplinary policy

Answer

Principles say what you want to achieve, and what actions are subject to the policy. Process itemizes steps, and responses itemize actions that result in automatic termination. Provisos include information about employment at will.

When an employee is in a disciplinary situation, he will be able to refer to the policy and know what he may expect. Also, when Bill is managing such a situation, he will be able to use this part of the policy as a reference.

As in this example, Bill can use this section of the policy to record situations in which it is acceptable to follow a course that is not within the boundaries set by the policy.

By recording what he is trying to achieve through the policy, Bill will be empowering his employees with a clear understanding of what their goals as an organization are.

Details and specificity give Bill a standard from which to work, and allow uncomfortable decisions to be based on the policy, instead of an impromptu judgment call at the time the action occurs.

By including this in the policy, Bill is clarifying what he expects of his employees.

A disciplinary policy is needed to ensure that the proceedings are fair and consistent to each employee. By publicizing your policy, and adhering to it, you will achieve this goal.

Disciplining effectively

Disciplining effectively

Effective discipline is always preceded by effective preparation. You must ensure that you are thorough and meticulous in preparing for any disciplinary proceeding that you have to carry out, if it is to be successful.

Some managers, like Lester and Carol, have not heeded the lesson that effective preparation leads to effective disciplinary actions. And they have experienced negative results from this mistake.

Lester

"I decided to make an example of Joan. She was renowned as a poor time keeper. I called her in to discipline her, but she proved that her time keeping was just fine."

Carol

"I knew Declan had been warned about not wearing a hard hat. So when I saw him without one, I intended to suspend him. But there were no past warnings on his file."

As Lester and Carol show, effective preparation involves careful and controlled actions on behalf of the manager who is considering instigating disciplinary proceedings.

Investigation

You need evidence. Do not rely on rumor or unsubstantiated opinions. The investigation must be impartial, evidence-based, and only consider actions that are covered by policies about performance and behavior in your company. Ask human resources professionals in your organization for advice.

Documentation

Document every step of your investigation. You may have to provide evidence of all your actions, and the reasoning behind them, if the disciplinary action that might follow is challenged. You need documentary proof of all interactions with the worker about the performance problem.

Conduct

Disciplinary actions need to be conducted in strict accordance with your policy. This means that the worker will have to be informed clearly about what the procedure is, as well as his rights-- especially his right to be accompanied. When preparing, consider the employee's right to privacy.

Question

Alan employs a worker who he wants to discipline because of persistent rudeness to other colleagues. What actions does Alan need to take to ensure that he prepares effectively for the disciplinary proceedings?

Options:

1. Alan must thoroughly investigate the alleged rudeness to establish concrete facts about its occurrence.

2. Alan should ensure that throughout his investigations, and any other interactions with his employee, that he makes careful notes of all transactions.

3. Alan must get legal advice before he attempts to discipline his employee.

4. Alan should instigate disciplinary proceedings by following the company disciplinary policy exactly.

5. Alan should inform his manager that he is intending to instigate disciplinary proceedings against an employee.

Answer

Actually, effective preparation includes a thorough investigation, documenting every action, and following the company's disciplinary policy carefully.

Option 1: Correct. Alan's investigation must be based on fact. This will take effort on his part, because if he is not thorough and factual, he could be caught in a potential dispute.

Option 2: Correct. Documenting every action will protect Alan throughout the disciplinary proceedings. This will allow him to provide evidence and show his rationale, in case the disciplinary action is challenged.

Option 3: Incorrect. While Alan might determine that legal advice would be useful, doing so is not required before proceeding with disciplinary action.

Option 4: Correct. Adhering strictly to the policy will give Alan and his company the greatest degree of protection possible. It will also allow the employee to know what his rights are, and how he can expect things to proceed.

Option 5: Incorrect. Informing his manager is not one of the actions that Alan needs to take to prepare for the disciplinary action. The employee's privacy needs to be considered.

Disciplining a worker is a stressful episode for most managers, and this can result in some vital aspects of preparation being missed. It's important to remember the three main actions for effective preparation to discipline.

Investigation

You may need to interview the worker, and others, to establish the facts. Give them all time to make their points. Inform them that you are just gathering evidence at this stage. Maintain confidentiality, and inform them of the next stages.

Documentation

Check with human resources staff members to establish what has been the response to a similar infringement, and check the worker's records to ensure that she is told about previous responses--if any--to the problem behavior.

Conduct

Organize the disciplinary event as quickly as possible. Make sure that you make arrangements to conduct it as privately as possible. Consider involving others--such as human resources personnel--to support and verify your actions.

You must prepare to conduct the disciplinary event in relation to your company's policy, and ensure that general issues of confidentiality, and the right to be accompanied are covered.

Case Study: Question 1 of 3

Scenario

You hear about an incident that occurs in your department and you think you need to respond. Mary, one of the assembly line workers, refuses to obey an instruction from her supervisor. This is reported to you by another manager, who was told about it by one of his workers, who saw the incident. The supervisor in question has been called to an emergency, and is away from the plant. You have a standard disciplinary policy in your company. How would you prepare to act in relation to this incident?

Answer these questions, in order.

Question

How would you prepare for a disciplinary response to Mary's actions?

Options:

1. I would call Mary into my office, and discipline her immediately.

2. I would fully investigate the incident by interviewing Mary and other relevant parties.

3. I would speak to Mary about her actions in front of the rest of the team to show everybody that such behavior will not be tolerated.

4. All of my dealings with Mary would be confidential.

Answer

In fact, you need to prepare to discipline by completing a thorough and confidential investigation.

Option 1: Incorrect. If you haven't yet determined the facts, you could end up accusing Mary of something she didn't do.

Option 2: Correct. You will want to be sure that you have all the facts before taking action. It is very risky to take action without actually knowing what happened.

Option 3: Incorrect. Mary's right to confidentiality would be violated if she were to be publicly disciplined.

Option 4: Correct. The employee has the rights to both confidentiality and to be accompanied in the disciplinary proceedings.

Case Study: Question 2 of 3

When you interview Mary's supervisor, he is very angry at her behavior. He says that, this time, you must act firmly with her, and dismiss her. What should you do in continuing to prepare for disciplining Mary?

Options:

1. I should check Mary's personnel records to establish if she has been disciplined for this offense before.

2. I should support the supervisor by disciplining Mary as seriously as I can, short of dismissal.

3. I should check with human resources to discover what the usual disciplinary response is for this action.

4. I should dismiss Mary, because refusing to obey a supervisor warrants such a response.

5. I should keep thorough records of all of my transactions in managing the situation.

Answer

Actually, you need to check out all of the documentation on Mary's disciplinary record, and establish how similar cases have been handled. You must also keep thorough records yourself.

Option 1: Correct. Learning Mary's history can shape your plan on how to discipline her. You will want to know all you can, in order to make the best decisions.

Option 2: Incorrect. Taking action without proper research and documentation could result in an embarrassing situation for the company. This could also make legal action easier for Mary to pursue.

Option 3: Correct. By checking with human resources, you will be able to better construct your ideas on how to deal with the situation with Mary. This will provide a precedent from which you can work.

Option 4: Incorrect. Even though Mary's dismissal may be warranted, you still need to do your research and have proper documentation supporting your actions.

Option 5: Correct. By keeping a record, you will be supporting the actions that you take. Careful documentation that details your actions will support your company's position, should the discipline be challenged.

Case Study: Question 3 of 3

Your investigations have led you to believe that Mary should be disciplined. How should you prepare to conduct the disciplinary event?

Options:

1. I would let things settle down a bit before I actually disciplined Mary.

2. I would discipline her on her own to keep the matter confidential.

3. I would inform Mary of when I intended to discipline her, explain the procedure, and tell her of her right to be accompanied.

4. I would arrange support and advice for myself for the disciplinary event from the Human Resources department.

5. I would arrange the discipline event as quickly as possible.

Problem Performance Management

Answer

In fact, in preparing to conduct the event, you need to act as quickly as possible while still informing Mary about the process and her rights. You should consider human resources support for yourself as well.

Option 1: Incorrect. Waiting to deal with the situation lessens the impact of actions that you might take. The disciplinary action should take place as soon as possible.

Option 2: Incorrect. Confidentiality is good, but you may need to involve others. You will need to do your research and gather sufficient support for your actions.

Option 3: Correct. You are informing her of how the policy dictates that the process should proceed, as well as informing her of her rights.

Option 4: Correct. Gaining support will verify that you are correct in your assertions. Human resources can also give you counsel in the decisions that you will be making.

Option 5: Correct. It is important to arrange the event quickly, before the memory of the infraction fades in your mind or in Mary's mind.

Mary may well have needed disciplining, but to prepare effectively for this, you should have conducted an investigation to establish the true facts. This must be complemented by a thorough search of all documents relevant to the case, and you must also keep complete records of all that you have done. The disciplinary event should be handled as quickly as possible, in accordance with the disciplinary procedures, which state that Mary needs to be informed about the nature of the proceedings and her right to be accompanied.

Sorin Dumitrascu

Disciplinary proceedings are an uncomfortable experience for most managers. So make sure you organize and conduct them properly by preparing thoroughly.

The likely effects of legislation on discipline

The likely effects of legislation on discipline

Many employers think that because of the doctrine of employment-at-will, they can fire employees at any time, and for any reason. So discipline is easy. But those employers are wrong--some reasons for firing employees are illegal.

Employment-at-will is the major form of employment relationship, but employment contracts can be used to bind both employer and employee into a more controlled relationship. A contract is a deliberate act, but some employers find their actions limited by implied contracts. Also, the employment-at-will doctrine has other exceptions.

Implied contracts

A contract can be implied when oral and written statements, and the employer's conduct combine. A handbook may state that employment will only be terminated for "just cause." This, combined with a hiring official's oral comments, may create a restriction on termination.

Public policy

Under the public-policy exception to employment-at-will, an employee is wrongfully discharged when the termination is against an explicit public policy and duty. Public policy is hard to define. One example is an employee refusing to act illegally, and then being fired.

Breaches of good faith

Employers have a duty to treat their employees fairly. This means that an employer's decisions can be tested against the concept of "just cause," or that terminations made in bad faith are prohibited.

Discrimination

The most common complaint employees take to court is that they were fired for discriminatory reasons. In countries with federal civil rights acts, this legislation means that employers may not intentionally use race, skin color, gender, religion, or national origin as the basis for discipline.

These four employers have all experienced legal restrictions after disciplining employees, even though they thought that, because of the employment-at-will doctrine, they could dismiss employees as they chose.

Lester

"I fired Dick when we closed the store for major refurbishment. He claimed that, at his interview, I'd promised that I'd employ him as long as he did his job. Then, of course, he cited our personnel policy, which states that termination will only be for 'just cause'."

Jenny

Problem Performance Management

"Sue gave evidence that resulted in us getting a huge fine. So, of course, I fired her. I didn't want someone so disloyal in my employment. But she claimed that if she'd lied, it would have been perjury, so I had no right to fire her. And the court agreed with her!"

Todd

"This happened without my knowledge or consent. Jimmy worked for us for 18 years, and he was a good employee. A new manager took over his section and fired him. Jimmy took us to court, and I'm glad he did. We should have dealt with him fairly."

Hazel

"I was away at the time, but even so this should never have happened. Tom had a heart attack and bypass surgery. The human resources people feared that he'd have another attack and be unable to work, so they fired him. That was just such obvious discrimination."

Question

Many employers are sure that they have rights to fire employees at will. But this is not entirely true. Match each exception to the relevant statement to show how legislation can affect discipline.

Options:

A. implied contracts
B. public policy
C. breaches of good faith
D. discrimination

Targets:

1. when an employee refuses to act illegally
2. Federal civil rights legislation
3. when oral and written statements, and the employer's conduct combine

4. revokes terminations motivated by malice

Answer

Breaches of good faith prevent malice-driven terminations, and civil rights legislation prevents discrimination. Public policy supports employees who refuse to act illegally, and implied contracts combine oral and written statements with employers' conduct.

This exception protects the employee from being wrongfully terminated when the company has acted against public policy and duty. Requiring an employee to act illegally goes against public policy.

In countries with civil rights acts, legislation states that employers may not intentionally use race, skin color, gender, religion, or national origin as the basis for discipline.

While implied contracts are not written down, it is important to remember that they will still stand up in the courtroom. An employer should be aware of implied contracts that exist in their organization.

In order for an employee to be treated fairly, termination requires just cause, and cannot be executed in bad faith. Careful documentation will support the reasoning for terminations.

So, what identifies the possibility that your approach to discipline, and particularly termination, will be affected by legislation? For each of the four exceptions, there are some warning signs that you should look for.

Implied contracts

Elements that affect implied contracts may include a discipline policy that states your mandatory progressive approach to discipline; statements in employee handbooks that define any terms of employment; and any verbal promises made to employees about the same issues.

Public policy

Employees must be free to exercise their legal rights, for example, joining a union, or refusing to do something that is illegal. In many places, employees are protected if they report other workers' illegal conduct, or wrongdoing.

Breaches of good faith

As well as obviously malevolent actions, companies need to consider any misleading statements or deception about the true nature of the employment. Actions short of dismissal, but which prompt an employee to leave, may also be seen as breaches of good faith.

Discrimination

Discrimination is legally prohibited in many countries. Laws may also cover employment discrimination. Also, federal laws in many countries make it unlawful to fire a worker merely for asserting rights under those laws.

The application of these legal restrictions upon discipline are complex, and vary from place to place. You should always check out your exact situation with a legal professional before you impose the ultimate sanction of termination on an employee. Here are some examples of the way that courts have generally interpreted legislation that affects discipline, and in particular termination.

Implied contracts

In Pine River State Bank v. Mettilee, the court ruled that a disciplinary policy in the employee handbook was an implied contract. The company breached that contract when it did not follow the procedures outlined in it.

Breaches of good faith

In Kmart Corporation v. Ponsock, the jury found that Kmart terminated Ponsock, a tenured employee, to avoid having to pay him retirement benefits. This entitled the employee to recover for a bad-faith agreement.

Public policy

In Palmateer v. International Harvester Corp., the court ruled that firing an employee because he informed the law enforcement authorities about the illegal acts of a co-worker was unacceptable. An actionable claim was brought against the company.

Discrimination

Browning-Ferris, Inc. illegally fired an employee with Crohn's disease. They said that it feared that the disease, and her exposure to waste, would be life-threatening. The court ruled that this was discriminatory.

Case Study: Question 1 of 2

Scenario

For your convenience, the case study is repeated with each question.

The CEO of a large clothes manufacturing company asks you to analyze her employment-at-will arrangements, and report back with any aspect that may identify an exception to the employment-at- will doctrine. You learn that the company is considering firing a woman caught stealing, a man aged 35 who is considered too old to operate complex machinery, and another man because he told the police about drug abuse at work.You also sit in on a recruitment interview, and hear a company official saying to a married woman with children--who wants to take them to after-school activities--that the sales job requires only a little traveling, which is untrue. The candidate also asks about tenure, and is told to consult the company handbook which says, "After a six-month probationary period, an employee can expect to be employed as long as his or her work is performed satisfactorily."

Answer the questions, in order.

Question

In the three potential terminations that the company is planning, which do you consider to be possible exceptions to the employment-at-will doctrine that show the effects of legislation on discipline?

Options:

1. The 35 year old man cannot be legally fired because of his age.

2. The termination of an employee, because he has told the police about drug abuse, is against public policy.

3. In many countries, age discrimination only applies to employees over 40 years of age. The company is not acting illegally in firing this man under the employment-at-will doctrine.

4. It is against public policy to fire a woman for stealing.

Answer

In fact, the man who told the police about drug abuse should not be fired, and, in many countries, age discrimination applies to workers over 40 years of age.

Option 1: Incorrect. In many countries, the age at which a person starts being protected under age discrimination laws is 40 years.

Option 2: Correct. The employee reported the illegal actions of others to the police. Public policy in many countries dictates that this is not grounds for the employee's dismissal.

Option 3: Correct. Since the employee is only 35 years old, he is not protected by the discrimination laws referring to age.

Option 4: Incorrect. Instead of public policy, this is an implied contract issue. An implied contract results when written policy, oral statements, and an employer's actions converge.

Case Study: Question 2 of 2

How do you analyze the information you have gained from the recruitment interview and company handbook? Other sales people have told you that the job does require limited traveling, because the worker is expected to move to an area and live in a hotel there for several weeks.

Options:

1. The statement about traveling is a breach of good faith, because it is deceiving the candidate about the true nature of the job.

2. The statement from the company handbook creates an implied contract. It suggests that employees cannot be fired if they have completed the probationary period, without some warning that their work performance was poor.

3. The statement from the company handbook means that, in the employment-at-will agreement, both parties can terminate the employment after six months for any reason.

4. The statement about traveling is true, so there is no breach of good faith.

Answer

Actually, the recruiter has breached good faith by deception, and the statement from the employee handbook creates an implied contract.

Problem Performance Management

Option 1: Correct. The candidate has the right to accurate information about the company. If the company is deceptive in their representation of themselves, they are breaching a good faith agreement with the candidate.

Option 2: Correct. This is a sound example of an implied contract. Even though the policy is not explicitly spelled out, the suggestion fulfills the implied contract.

Option 3: Incorrect. The company handbook states that by meeting certain requirements, an employee cannot be terminated without first obtaining some notice of poor performance.

Option 4: Incorrect. The employer did not lie when they told the candidate that travel was limited. It is because they allowed her to believe that she would still be able to take her children to activities that it was a breach of good faith.

In this company, legislation can affect the disciplinary process because the company is acting against public policy by firing the worker who informs about drug abuse. But since the other worker is under 40 years of age, it is not legally discriminating against him.

The company is, however, guilty of a breach of good faith by deceiving the candidate about the true working conditions. And the employment handbook creates an implied contract about termination after the probationary period.

The impact of legislation is complex, and you should get professional advice about it. Nevertheless, you should now be aware that legislation in many countries does affect discipline, and this can lead to significant problems for companies.

Section 2 - The Conventional Progressive Disciplinary Approach

Section 2 - The Conventional Progressive Disciplinary Approach

Progressive discipline is the approach most organizations use to handle problem performers. Used effectively, it is a good tool for managing behavior in the workplace.

Verbal warnings--sometimes referred to as oral warnings--and written warnings are the first two stages in a progressive disciplinary approach. They are not punitive responses. They are, literally, intended to warn workers that their behaviors are unacceptable.

They are also a warning of a potentially escalating response. They clearly show the progressive nature of this approach to discipline.

Suspension is usually, but not always, the third stage in a progressive disciplinary approach. Because the impact of suspension is so much greater then administering a warning, it is a much more serious step.

Suspension means being sent off the job for a period of time. It is a serious measure with significant consequences for the employee, and the company. So you need to be entirely sure that it is an appropriate response. If you are going to suspend someone, you must do so effectively, and you must be prepared for the consequences of this act.

Termination is, of course, the most serious response to problem performance in the workplace. As such, it should not be taken lightly or without due attention to detail.

Termination will usually occur as a result of a single and very serious act of misconduct by an employee, or because of a conduct problem that persists over time, despite all of your best efforts to correct it. In either case, the seriousness of the response demands that you are particularly thorough in the way that you establish that such a course of action is appropriate. There are three parts to establishing appropriateness.

The conventional progressive approach to discipline

Progressive discipline is the approach most organizations use to handle problem performers. Used effectively, it is a good tool for managing behavior in the workplace.

Progressive discipline is an escalating response to workplace behavior problems. It begins with a warning, but then moves on to more punitive responses if the worker does not improve, or if the original infraction warrants a more severe punishment. The usual stages in the process are:
- a verbal warning,
- a written warning,
- suspension from work,
- termination.

This approach, therefore, can offer a range of responses to problem performance. Workers know where they are on a sequential scale, and the escalating responses allow for improvement. The benefits of this approach are:
- it is flexible enough to respond to minor and major infractions,
- it gives plenty of opportunity for workers who want to improve their behaviors,
- it is progressive, so workers can easily understand the escalating consequences if they don't remedy their behaviors.

Both Nathan and Rachel have experienced the progressive discipline system in their organizations. And although it was a difficult time for them, they both found the system helped them in the end.

Nathan

"I thought the disciplinary system only dealt with serious offenses. But it helped me stop my repeated lateness, by giving me a time frame in which to correct my behavior."

Rachel

"I finally realized how serious matters were when my manager told me that my lack of improvement meant that I was to get a written warning."

But although Rachel and Nathan responded to the progressive discipline approach, and remedied their behaviors, not every one will. So you cannot, and should not, avoid using the final sanction of termination in dealing with some employees.

But with such a progressive system, you can feel assured that you have given workers every opportunity to improve their behaviors before you have to dismiss them from your employment.

Question

Roy was reluctant to become a manager because he feared having to discipline some of his old colleagues. What are the benefits of applying the progressive approach to discipline?

Options:

1. The approach provides plenty of opportunity for workers to improve, if they want to.

2. The approach means that you can avoid terminating employees.

3. It is a flexible approach, enabling you to respond to minor and major infractions.

4. The approach is progressive, and workers can easily understand the escalating consequences, if they don't remedy their behaviors.

5. All workers will respond to this approach.

Answer

Actually, the benefits of the progressive disciplinary approach lie in its flexibility, opportunity for workers to improve, and its escalating nature.

Option 1: Correct. Using a progressive disciplinary approach allows employees to receive ample notification that they need to change their behavior.

Option 2: Incorrect. Termination is the last option in the progressive approach. If an employee is unwilling to change, it could result in her termination.

Option 3: Correct. This flexibility allows you the greatest amount of control over disciplinary situations.

Problem Performance Management

Option 4: Correct. The progressive approach will allow you to rely on the policy, saving you from having to make up rules as the situation escalates.

Option 5: Incorrect. Some workers may have no desire to change their behavior. Ultimately, this could lead to their dismissal.

As a manager, you cannot be effective unless you maintain discipline among your team. Applying the progressive disciplinary approach provides you with a simple and effective way of operating at this difficult time.

Administering verbal and written warnings

Administering verbal and written warnings

Verbal warnings--sometimes referred to as oral warnings--and written warnings are the first two stages in a progressive disciplinary approach. They are not punitive responses. They are, literally, intended to warn workers that their behaviors are unacceptable.

They are also a warning of a potentially escalating response. They clearly show the progressive nature of this approach to discipline.

A verbal warning usually, but not always, comes before a written warning. It is the beginning of the disciplinary process. If a verbal warning is not responded to, then a manager may choose to move on to a written warning. A verbal warning implies that it is spoken, but it is insufficient to merely tell workers that their behavior is unacceptable.

Verbal warnings

Problem Performance Management

You tell an employee that you are dissatisfied with her workplace performance. It is a formal process, which must be recorded. It is appropriate for the first instances of minor rule violations, or performance lapses. You may give more than one verbal warning.

Written warnings

This is for workers not responding after a verbal warning, or for repeated violation of a minor work rule. It may be the first response to a violation of a more major work rule. It explains expected improvements, and the consequences of failure.

Both verbal and written warnings rely on deciding how serious the worker's offense is. They are usually appropriate for more minor offenses. Among other behaviors, minor offenses could include:

- foul language,
- smoking,
- tardiness,
- poor productivity.

Monica

Monica was 15 minutes late for the start of her shift. The supervisor checked that she did not have any legitimate excuse for this lateness, and then verbally warned her that such behavior was unacceptable.

Nancy

Her supervisor had checked that Nancy would be able to complete the report by the end of the day. When she didn't, and had no legitimate explanation for her failure, the supervisor gave her a verbal warning.

Terry

Terry had been verbally warned about smoking in the building. On the second time that he was discovered to be smoking at his desk, his manager gave him a written warning.

Nick

Nick completely lost his temper, and started yelling at a customer. Although this was the first time he had done such a thing, his team leader felt that the behavior warranted an immediate written warning.

Question

Desmond had to respond to a worker who he felt needed disciplining. But he was unsure of the distinction between a verbal and written warning. Help him by identifying which statements are true.

Options:

1. An oral warning is the same as a written warning.

2. A verbal warning is usually appropriate for a first-time, minor offense.

3. A verbal warning has to be recorded.

4. A written warning may be an appropriate response for the first-time violation of a more major work rule.

5. A written warning is not appropriate if the worker has already had some verbal warnings.

6. A written warning usually comes after a verbal warning.

Answer

In fact, a verbal warning usually comes before a written warning. It is appropriate for first-time, minor offenses, and has to be recorded. A written warning may be appropriate for the first-time violation of a more major work rule.

Option 1: Incorrect. A written warning sends a stronger message to the employee. However, Desmond should reserve the written warning for either major infractions or repeated behavior.

Option 2: Correct. Desmond's verbal warning simply notifies the employee that their behavior is not acceptable and that it should change.

Option 3: Correct. It is important for Desmond to have a record of verbal warnings that have been issued, in case of dispute.

Option 4: Correct. A written warning carries more weight and communicates a stronger message from Desmond to the employee. It is appropriate for more serious infractions.

Option 5: Incorrect. Desmond can issue multiple verbal warnings without moving on to a written one. The written warning should be used in the cases of repeated offenses or major infractions.

Option 6: Correct. Progressively moving from a verbal warning to a written one allows employees to improve their behavior if they choose to.

Giving an employee either a verbal or written warning is obviously a serious matter. So to make sure that you are doing it as effectively as possible, you need to follow these guidelines.

Delivering a verbal warning

Adopt a serious tone. Don't deviate or praise another aspect of the employee's work. Hold the meeting in private, but let the worker be accompanied if she chooses. Explain the problem, your expectations, and the consequences. Ask for the worker's views. Keep notes.

Delivering a written warning

Give the written warning and get a receipt. The warning should include a statement of misconduct, the work rule violated, past misconduct, expected improvement, and consequences. Let the worker be accompanied. Discuss the contents and an improvement plan with the worker.

Case Study: Question 1 of 2
Scenario

Darren has ignored your instruction to keep his work area tidy. Desks must be cleared, and work correctly stored at the end of each working day. This is company policy, and is stated clearly in the company handbook issued to all employees. You have instructed him to tidy up twice in the last week, and he does not seem to have done anything about it. You are considering disciplining Darren.

Answer these questions, in order, to demonstrate how you will proceed.

Question

How will you discipline Darren? Which statements would you make to Darren?

Options:

1. "Darren, I know you work really hard and are busy, but you have to keep a tidy desk."

2. "Darren, your failure to keep your desk tidy, in spite of my warnings, is against company policy. Do you have any explanation?"

3. "Darren, this is a verbal warning. You must leave your desk tidy at the end of the day. If this happens again, I will consider giving you a written warning."

4. "Darren, I'm warning you. Keep your desk tidy, or else!"

5. "Darren, I'm going to keep written notes of this warning, and keep it on your file."

Answer

In fact, to administer a verbal warning to Darren, you should be clear, direct, and your tone serious. You should seek an explanation from him, and explain the consequences if his behavior does not improve. You should keep notes.

Option 1: Incorrect. It is important to adopt a more formal tone than this, and not include positive feedback. Darren needs to realize that this warning is serious, and will not be ignored by you.

Option 2: Correct. This statement formally addresses Darren, reminds him of repeated warnings in the past, and gives him the opportunity to explain his actions.

Option 3: Correct. By saying this, you have clearly informed Darren that you are issuing a verbal warning. You are also communicating that repeated behavior will result in progressive discipline.

Option 4: Incorrect. This response doesn't allow Darren the opportunity to explain his actions. Also, it doesn't inform him that this is a verbal warning that will be recorded, or that further infractions may result in a written warning.

Option 5: Correct. Keeping a record of the incident will help document what actually happened as well as provide support in the case of a dispute. Alerting Darren to the record-keeping may encourage him to comply.

Case Study: Question 2 of 2

Darren does not respond to your verbal warning. You administer a written warning to him. Which extracts would be appropriate for a written warning?

Options:

1. You failed to leave your desk tidy at the end of each day. This is against company policy, as stated in the handbook.

2. We've had complaints from other workers about the untidy state of your desk.

3. On June 6th, you were verbally warned about your behavior.

4. Failure to leave your desk tidy in the future will result in suspension.

5. Sign and return this copy of the warning as confirmation of your receipt.

6. A copy of this warning will be put on the department notice board.

Answer

Actually, a written warning should include a statement of misconduct, the work rule violated, past misconduct, expected improvement, and the consequences if no improvement is made. It should also incorporate a receipt.

Option 1: Correct. Stating the inappropriate behavior and pointing out that it is against company policy are both important components of a written warning. Your message to Darren is clear.

Option 2: Incorrect. The written warning focuses on the infraction, the rule it violated, past history, how the behavior should improve, and consequences if it doesn't improve. Collecting information is part of a verbal warning.

Option 3: Correct. A written warning is more effective if it includes reminders of past misconduct and warnings. Darren may reconsider his choices when reminded of the frequency of his actions.

Problem Performance Management

Option 4: Correct. It is vital to include notice of future consequences if the misbehavior continues. This allows the employee to take responsibility for his actions and also protects the company in case of dispute.

Option 5: Correct. The final element of a written warning is obtaining a written receipt from the employee, acknowledging that they received and understood the contents of the warning.

Option 6: Incorrect. The written warning should be delivered in person and a receipt should be received. The employee's confidentiality should be considered, but they should be informed of their right to an acquaintance.

Darren's verbal warning should be delivered in a serious tone. It should be straightforward, direct, and seek any explanation from him about his behavior. The warning should include a statement about expected behavior, and the consequences if Darren fails to improve.

The written warning should include a statement of Darren's misconduct, the work rule violated, his past misconduct, expected improvement, and the consequences if he does not improve. It must also incorporate a receipt.

Issuing any sort of disciplinary warning demands that you behave professionally and properly. Follow these guidelines, and you will manage this difficult task effectively.

Using suspension as part of a disciplinary response

Using suspension as part of a disciplinary response

Suspension is usually, but not always, the third stage in a progressive disciplinary approach. Because the impact of suspension is so much greater then administering a warning, it is a much more serious step.

Suspension means being sent off the job for a period of time. It is a serious measure with significant consequences for the employee, and the company. So you need to be entirely sure that it is an appropriate response. If you are going to suspend someone, you must do so effectively, and you must be prepared for the consequences of this act.

The appropriateness of suspension

Suspension may lead to termination. It is a response to serious behaviors that may, or may not, be illegal. Examples are using drugs, fighting, stealing, religious, sexual, or racial harassment. You may suspend for a lesser offense--already disciplined to no effect, or to investigate.

The details of suspension

You can suspend with, or without, pay. Obviously, the latter has much more impact. Generally, you can't suspend salaried employees without pay, but you can suspend hourly-paid workers. You must consider the impact on the worker and on the workplace to determine the term of the suspension.

Arrangements while on suspension

How will the suspended employee's work be managed? You need to consider the worker's e-mail account, computer access, credit cards, and access to the building. You should inform co-workers without breaching confidentiality, and tell them to make no work-related contact.

Rocky, Elle, Barry, and Petra have all been suspended from work. Their situations are typical of the reasons for suspending an employee. Their suspensions also show how the details of the act itself, and the arrangements for managing while they were suspended, had to be organized.

Rocky

Elle repeatedly smoked on site, and even though she was formally warned, did not change her behavior. Her suspension was for one day with pay, as she was a salaried employee. Her work was easily shared among her colleagues.

Elle

Rocky hit his supervisor when confronted about his lateness. He was suspended for three days without pay. Security was informed, and Rocky's access to the site was also suspended. His colleagues were told about the suspension the same day.

Barry

Barry was accused by a co-worker of taking drugs. He was immediately suspended so that the alleged incident could be investigated. The allegation was unfounded, and Barry was immediately reinstated.

Petra

Petra was accused of stealing money from her co-workers. She was immediately suspended. The investigation proved that she had done so, and her employment was terminated.

Question

Lawrence was considering suspending an employee. He felt that this was a major step, so he checked out the main elements he needed to consider to manage the suspension effectively with the human resources department. What should they have told him?

Options:

1. You can't suspend someone if you haven't already given that person a written warning.

2. You can suspend workers over serious allegations while you investigate their behaviors.

3. You can suspend with or without pay.

4. You should inform the suspended employee's co-workers, but without breaching any confidentiality.

5. You cannot refuse the suspended worker access to the work site.

Answer

Actually, you can suspend to investigate an appropriate issue, and suspensions can be with, or without, pay. Co-workers need to be informed about the suspension, but confidentiality must be maintained.

Option 1: Incorrect. Depending on the nature of the infraction, a suspension might be the first intervention. Lawrence should consider this case separate from all others.

Option 2: Correct. This way Lawrence can find the truth of the matter before having to make a decision as to whether or not to reinstate the employee.

Option 3: Correct. In deciding to suspend the employee with or without pay, Lawrence will consider the nature of the infraction--or alleged infraction.

Option 4: Correct. The employee's confidentiality is very important. However, Lawrence should inform necessary co-workers, because the employee's absence will impact them.

Option 5: Incorrect. A suspended worker should be kept from anything that deals with the workplace. Lawrence will need to address all the arrangements that should be made in the employee's absence.

The method of handling a suspension follows the general pattern that is used for administering any disciplinary action. You need to:

- deliver the suspension notice personally, and in confidence,
- allow workers to be accompanied, if they so choose,
- explain the violation, the relationship to company rules, and the consequences of any repetition of the behavior,
- detail your expectations about future behavior.

A serious act

Explain that because of the seriousness of the employee's action, you are leaving out the earlier steps. You must stress why the behavior is so unacceptable, and ensure that the worker understands that a repetition will usually result in termination.

No improvement

Establish the history of problems, and attempts made to deal with the matter before. Explain that suspension is to bring home the gravity of the offense. Offer support, if the worker seems receptive, in helping the employee to improve.

Investigation

Explain that suspension is not a punishment. Suspend with pay. Investigate issues that, if proved, must not be allowed to continue, and where the facts need detailed clarification. Don't imply any conclusion to the investigation.

Suspension is a very serious disciplinary response. It has a major impact upon the individual, and the company, so it is vital that it is handled correctly to have the desired effect.

Termination as part of a progressive disciplinary approach

Termination as part of a progressive disciplinary approach

Termination is, of course, the most serious response to problem performance in the workplace. As such, it should not be taken lightly or without due attention to detail.

Termination will usually occur as a result of a single and very serious act of misconduct by an employee, or because of a conduct problem that persists over time, despite all of your best efforts to correct it. In either case, the seriousness of the response demands that you are particularly thorough in the way that you establish that such a course of action is appropriate. There are three parts to establishing appropriateness.

Seriousness

Does the problem warrant this response? Is it dangerous to others, illegal or damaging to your business? Will you be liable as a result? If it is a cumulative performance problem, has it been through the previous stages without an improvement in behavior?

Conduct

Have you conducted yourself properly? Unless they are admitted, have you established the true facts by investigation? Are any previous interventions properly recorded? Have you sought a second opinion, preferably a legal opinion?

Challenges

Can you be challenged? Was the employee aware that such behavior was against company policy, and could lead to termination? Have you made any verbal statements to contradict policies? Has equivalent behavior warranted termination?

The seriousness of the action taken by an employee is always open to interpretation. But there are several areas where things are more clear cut.

Terminations are difficult. But if you have satisfied yourself that terminating an employee is the only right course of action, then you are justified in taking the action.

Sandy, Neil, and Helen have all terminated employees. Although they were not pleased that they had done it, they were pleased it was for the right reasons, and in the right way.

Sandy

"I knew that I had no choice, and that termination was the only possible response. Ryan expressed racist remarks about a customer. Neither the company, nor I, will tolerate such behavior. He was heard by other colleagues, and after consultation with our legal people, I dismissed him."

Neil

"Don denied taking drugs. But the random urine sample tested positive. I immediately suspended him, and then investigated. His locker contained illegal substances. I checked, and this sort of behavior always resulted in instant dismissal. So that's what I did."

Helen

"I made absolutely sure that Serena knew the speed limit for forklifts. The signs showed the limit. She was properly trained, and her supervisor had reminded her of the rule only that week. But she still drove so fast as to put her colleagues in real danger. I think she had to be dismissed."

Question

Eric is considering firing an employee. He has been to see his colleagues in the human resources department and they have given him a list of questions to ask himself, to make sure that he is behaving appropriately. Which questions should be on that list?

Options:

1. Are any previous disciplinary interventions for this employee properly recorded?

2. Have you allowed the employee access to legal representatives in work time?

3. Have you sought a second opinion about terminating this worker?

4. Have you made any verbal statements to contradict policies that may justify the employee's behavior?

5. In your team, has equivalent behavior warranted termination?

6. Are the employee's records stored confidentially?

Answer

Actually, you must establish the true, disciplinary record, and seek a second opinion about termination. You must ensure that no verbal statements have been made which contradict policy, and check on equivalent responses.

Option 1: Correct. By researching this, Eric can know if the employee's behavior is repeated, even with previous attempts at discipline. Answering this question will shape Eric's decision whether or not to suspend the employee.

Option 2: Incorrect. Eric shouldn't have this question on his list because this is not something he needs to worry about. He is under no obligation to provide the employee with access to counsel on the company's time.

Option 3: Correct. Doing this bolsters Eric's argument for dismissing the employee. If the person giving the second opinion agrees, then Eric's decision is further validated.

Option 4: Correct. Looking critically at his own behavior, searching for mixed messages, might cause Eric to better understand the employee's behavior. It could also help Eric avoid potential disputes.

Option 5: Correct. This gives appropriate balance for not only the employee, but for the entire team. Eric has a standard by which he can judge his own actions.

Option 6: Incorrect. The confidentiality of the employee must be respected, but it is not one of the questions that needs to be on his checklist.

Problem Performance Management

Sometimes, however, termination is inappropriate. If the company is wrong in firing a worker, this may result in a lawsuit with significant costs.

Andrew

Andrew fired a worker he knew had been disciplined for repeated lateness. But the case fell apart when the employee proved that there were no written records of any verbal or written warnings in regard to his promptness.

Pete

Pete knew that Emma was guilty of stealing because she had a criminal record. He asked her co-workers, and they all felt sure she had done it. But she challenged the dismissal, because there was no real proof that she had stolen anything.

Cathy

Cathy denied it, but witnesses confirmed that she had told Tim that he didn't need to wear a hard hat all the time. This verbal contradiction of company policy meant he successfully challenged his dismissal for not following safety procedures.

Matthew

Matthew dismissed Sue for bringing alcohol into the office. She challenged him, and proved that on the last three times that disciplinary action had been taken for the same issue, the workers had been given written warnings for a first offense.

Andrew relied on his knowledge of previous disciplinary actions. He should have checked the personnel records thoroughly. Pete conducted a perfunctory investigation, and this meant that his disciplinary action was based on a faulty premise. Cathy had forgotten that verbal statements can contradict, or at least confuse, written policies. Matthew did not check that his actions were in accord with previous responses to this behavior in the company. They all failed to attend sufficiently to the detail in their respective situations.

Damon's employment can be appropriately terminated because he has committed a sufficiently serious offense to warrant termination. His actions have been thoroughly investigated, and the second opinion verified the decision to terminate. But Cathy's termination would not be appropriate. She had been given verbal permission, and equivalent offenses had received a warning. Sol's cumulative failure to improve his behavior merits termination. With the records and investigation, his termination would be appropriate.

Termination is the most serious response to misconduct in the workplace. As such, it merits the most serious effort on your behalf to ensure that you are acting appropriately.

Section 3 - Alternatives to the Conventional Approach to Discipline at Work

Section 3 - Alternatives to the Conventional Approach to Discipline at Work

Discipline has an inflexible feel to it. Rules may change, but the fundamental exercise of control through discipline remains constant. But today, everything is open to change, and even discipline can be challenged and reinterpreted.

The conventional, progressive, and some would emphasize, punitive approach to discipline in the workplace is quite an old-fashioned system. Alternative models have been proposed, which take a more positive and less punishing approach to controlling the workforce.

The conventional approach to discipline at work has critics. It has been the most popular approach to discipline since the 1930's. But some writers suggest it is inappropriate for the 21st century, and the current workforce.

Dick Grote, one of the strongest critics of the conventional approach to discipline states, "Our analysis indicated that there were virtually no benefits we could attribute to the old system, other than its rarely needed ability to allow us to prove that the individual had received a measure of 'due process' should our decision to fire him later be challenged."

The most cogent alternative to the conventional progressive approach to discipline is usually referred to as the positive approach to discipline.

Positive discipline is a response to the criticisms of the conventional approach to discipline, and offers a contrasting model. There are four major characteristics of this approach: the underlying assumptions behind the approach; the emphasis of the approach; how problems are dealt with; and the role of the supervisor.

Discipline without Punishment is the form of positive discipline developed by Dick Grote. According to him, it is a proven strategy that turns problem employees into superior performers.

The State of Georgia decided to implement the Discipline without Punishment system in every agency throughout the state. Two years later, surveys were sent to the personnel officers and supervisors of those agencies to learn how well the program had served them. The overwhelming majority of managers and supervisors reported very positive results.

The system emphasizes a coaching activity--as opposed to counseling--taken by supervisors when problem performance is identified. This establishes that the worker understands the performance problem, and agrees to remedy it. The principle is that the worker is reminded of his personal responsibility for performance. If there is no improvement, reminders are given before the final chance for the worker to improve is given. This is called decision-making leave. Coaching and decision-making leave are the unique elements in Discipline without Punishment.

Alternative approaches to discipline

Alternative approaches to discipline

Discipline has an inflexible feel to it. Rules may change, but the fundamental exercise of control through discipline remains constant. But today, everything is open to change, and even discipline can be challenged and reinterpreted.

The conventional, progressive, and some would emphasize, punitive approach to discipline in the workplace is quite an old-fashioned system. Alternative models have been proposed, which take a more positive and less punishing approach to controlling the workforce.

These approaches are characterized as being more in tune with contemporary employment relationships. In this view, workers must be more responsible for their own actions, and for correcting their own performance.

Both systems are used today by organizations. But whether you choose to keep to the conventional,

progressive approach, or change to the positive approach, it is of benefit to have alternatives. You have:
- a variety of possible approaches to choose from,
- the opportunity to justify the merits of your approach when it's compared to alternatives,
- the opportunity to take elements from alternatives in formulating your unique approach.

In the article, "A positive approach to workplace problems; why the State of Florida should adopt it now!" Stephen. K. Foster points out that, "the Florida legislature created an historic opportunity to assess the State's approach to managing performance and behavioral problems." Hence his article.

But Dave Green, personnel manager at Platte River Authority, quoted in Personnel Journal, says that they tried positive discipline. It didn't work, and his organization has gone back to the more conventional approach.

Of course, system change can be disruptive and confusing. It will take considerable time and effort on your behalf to implement a new approach. But these are poor reasons for not exploring the alternatives.

Question

Ruby is the personnel manager at a large electronics company. The company has been troubled by performance and behavior problems, and she wants the senior management team to consider alternatives to its present approach to discipline. What are the benefits that she could cite for considering alternative approaches?

Options:

1. "We can spend considerable time exploring the alternatives."

2. "We will have a range of approaches to choose from."

3. "We will have to justify the merits of whatever approach we take."

4. "The change will do the workforce good."

5. "We can construct our own approach with elements from the alternatives we consider."

Answer

In fact, the benefits of considering alternative disciplinary approaches are that it increases the possible choices, it will make you justify the merits of your choice, and you can develop your own unique approach.

Option 1: Incorrect. The team will benefit from using their time efficiently to find an alternative approach.

Option 2: Correct. Ruby can explain that the variety is useful in determining discipline strategies. The approach can be specifically matched to meet the needs of the individual employees.

Option 3: Correct. Examining the alternatives can provide additional information regarding the approach that Ruby's company takes. This could shape their perception of their present system, as well as any new programs they decide to implement.

Option 4: Incorrect. The senior managers are interested in tangible benefits to the company. Change just for the sake of change does not provide that.

Option 5: Correct. By doing this the company can create a "custom" approach that meets their own unique needs.

Change is not always good, but at least you should keep up-to-date with the latest approaches to discipline, and compare them with your existing methods. Then you will be able to find the best approach for you.

The main criticisms of the conventional approach to

discipline at work

The main criticisms of the conventional approach to discipline at work

The conventional approach to discipline at work has critics. It has been the most popular approach to discipline since the 1930's. But some writers suggest it is inappropriate for the 21st century, and the current workforce.

Dick Grote, one of the strongest critics of the conventional approach to discipline states, "Our analysis indicated that there were virtually no benefits we could attribute to the old system, other than its rarely needed ability to allow us to prove that the individual had received a measure of 'due process' should our decision to fire him later be challenged."

Out of step

"Progressive discipline is out of step with the needs and culture of today's organizations." Stephen K. Foster.

Resentful

"Employees who are punished for misbehavior haven't become more productive workers. Instead, many become resentful--or sneaky so they don't get caught." Joan Lloyd.

Criticisms of the conventional, progressive disciplinary approach center around three main themes. They are that the approach is adversarial; that it is expensive; and that it is ineffective.

Adversarial

It creates an adversarial relationship between supervisor and employee. The supervisor becomes a disciplinarian, and many supervisors are uncomfortable with that role and are reluctant to use it, until it is too late.

Expensive

It is punitive, so workers are likely to defend themselves. Appeals are common, and the process escalates. Lawyers get involved, and it becomes expensive and time consuming. Supervisors avoid disciplining for this reason.

Ineffective

It is based on the contradiction of punishing, but also improving, behavior. Punishment is unsuccessful at improving behavior, except in the short term. Warnings are ignored, and suspension usually leads to termination, achieving nothing.

Brian, Penny, and Roy are three managers who have not found the conventional, progressive disciplinary approach effective in their workplaces.

Brian

"For most of my time at work, I'm talking to my team about empowerment and responsibility. Then I'm supposed to stop that approach, and come down heavily on them with a punishment if they don't behave. That just doesn't work for me. I'm a facilitator, not a disciplinarian."

Penny

"If disciplinary action is mentioned, I run a mile. I'm too busy to get bogged down in all of those interviews, evidence gathering, and hearings. And I know if the legal people get involved, it's going to drag on for months, and every tiny incident will have to be examined in minute detail."

Roy

"I warned one of my team members for being late, but it made no difference. So then I suspended him without pay. That got his attention, but it didn't change his behavior. He just got a lot more clever at playing the system. Now he always rings up with an excuse. I think he's just laughing at me."

Question

Toby was not convinced of the benefits of the conventional approach to discipline used in his workplace. What are the main criticisms of this approach?

Options:

1. It is expensive and time consuming, because the punitive nature of the approach means that employees are likely to defend themselves.

2. It is ineffective, because employees today do not accept the authority of their supervisors.

3. It creates an adversarial relationship between supervisor and employee, which makes many supervisors reluctant to use it.

4. The contradiction of punishing, but also improving behavior, is irreconcilable, and so is ineffective in both cases.

5. It is based on a judicial system.

Answer

In fact, the criticisms of the conventional approach to discipline center around its adversarial nature, its expensiveness, and its lack of effectiveness.

Option 1: Correct. Managers like Toby will be reluctant to use a conventional approach because they feel it causes more problems than it solves.

Option 2: Incorrect. The doubt is caused by the incongruity between punishing and improving. The perception of authority does not necessarily relate to this issue.

Option 3: Correct. Toby wants healthy working relationships with the other employees. However, when employees and managers are at odds with each other, this is not possible.

Option 4: Correct. Toby feels that when people think they are being punished, they may be inclined to ignore warnings or find other ways to get around the rules."

Option 5: Incorrect. The argument against the conventional approach focuses on its adversarial nature, its potential and actual expenses, and questionable results.

The conventional approach to discipline has some powerful critics. Now you are in a position to make up your mind about whether you agree, or disagree with them.

A positive approach to discipline

A positive approach to discipline

The most cogent alternative to the conventional progressive approach to discipline is usually referred to as the positive approach to discipline.

Positive discipline is a response to the criticisms of the conventional approach to discipline, and offers a contrasting model. There are four major characteristics of this approach: the underlying assumptions behind the approach; the emphasis of the approach; how problems are dealt with; and the role of the supervisor.

Assumptions

Most employees actually want to do a good job, and all they really need is an occasional reminder, and support. The relationship between employees and managers is not adversarial, and confrontational. It is consensual, and empowering.

Emphasis

Problem Performance Management

The emphasis of this approach is on problem solving, as opposed to the punishment emphasis of the conventional approach. And, crucially, the responsibility for the behavior and the improvement of that behavior, rests with the worker.

Problems

Problem behavior is not punished. Counseling support is offered to workers to help them solve the problems. Some firms use decision-making leave to enable workers to confirm their willingness to improve. Only if they will not, is dismissal an option.

Supervisors

Supervisors are not in a punitive role in this approach. They are counselors, coaches, and facilitators. These are roles congruent with their general relationship with workers. Supervisors communicate standards, monitor performance, and support.

Many organizations are now adopting disciplinary procedures that are more in accord with the positive approach. Julie, Heather, Gordon, and Kirk all work in companies where the positive approach to discipline is applied.

Julie

"When I couldn't manage to keep up with the required output, my boss talked with me about what I needed to do, and what he could do to help. This felt wonderful. In my last job, they would have just assumed I was lazy, and given me a warning. Here, they assumed I was trying as hard as I could."

Heather

"I had some trouble with promptness. So I was expecting the usual reprimand from my boss. But he just accepted my excuse, and focused on what I would do to make sure it didn't happen again. He just assumed that it was something that I should, and could, resolve--so I have."

Gordon

"I had some trouble controlling my temper, particularly with difficult customers. I was given a day off work to sort myself out, and to work out how I was going to resolve the problem. Some people might think this was just a holiday, but for me, it really helped me to get my attitude to work right."

Kirk

"My supervisor is a real help to me. In the last place I worked, all supervisors did was shout at the workers. Here, they see their role as supporting, and counseling. When I had some attitude problems, my supervisor was wonderful in getting me to sit down, and think them through."

Organizations rarely follow exact blueprints in designing and implementing policy, particularly in something as individual as disciplinary procedures. So your organization may have a mix of the characteristics of positive, and conventional approaches to discipline.

Question

Jo works in an organization that says that it employs a positive approach to discipline. She is not sure what this means. Identify the characteristics of the positive approach to discipline.

Options:

1. Confrontational and oppositional are the dominant styles.

2. Consensus and empowerment are the key attitudes.

3. Coaching and counseling are the methods for dealing with problems.
4. Employees are punished for any wrongdoing.
5. Responsibility is vested in the employee.
6. Supervisors communicate standards, monitor performance, and support.

Answer

Actually, the characteristics of the positive approach include consensus and empowerment, the use of coaching and counseling, responsibility vested in the worker, and supervisors being communicators and monitors of standards.

Option 1: Incorrect. The positive approach avoids confrontation by using methods that are not so punishing, to motivate employees to demonstrate good behavior.

Option 2: Correct. The positive approach assumes that, for the most part, employees want to be good performers. At times, they need extra support and motivation, but this can be done in a positive manner.

Option 3: Correct. Under the positive approach, managers can step out of the role of disciplinarian and administrator of punishment. Rather, they are problem solvers and teachers to the people they manage.

Option 4: Incorrect. The positive approach focuses on upbeat strategies. Punishment is not regarded as the method of choice for improving employees' behavior.

Option 5: Correct. The positive approach requires an employee to accept responsibilities that lead to their own success. This motivates the employees to be more active in their career development.

Option 6: Correct. The positive approach allows supervisors to be communicators and supporters, rather than judges and enforcers.

The positive approach to discipline is increasingly advocated as being more appropriate for contemporary organizations. You must be aware of the approach, and consider how applicable it is for your company.

Discipline without Punishment

Discipline without Punishment

Discipline without Punishment is the form of positive discipline developed by Dick Grote. According to him, it is a proven strategy that turns problem employees into superior performers.

The State of Georgia decided to implement the Discipline without Punishment system in every agency throughout the state. Two years later, surveys were sent to the personnel officers and supervisors of those agencies to learn how well the program had served them. The overwhelming majority of managers and supervisors reported very positive results.

The system emphasizes a coaching activity--as opposed to counseling--taken by supervisors when problem performance is identified. This establishes that the worker understands the performance problem, and agrees to remedy it. The principle is that the worker is reminded of his personal responsibility for performance. If there is no improvement, reminders are given before the final chance for the worker to improve is given. This is called decision-making leave. Coaching and decision-making leave are the unique elements in Discipline without Punishment.

Coaching

This is a planned discussion with the goal of improving performance. The supervisor's role is to make performance expectations clear and precise. The coaching session should result in the employee agreeing to improve his behavior.

Decision-making leave

This part of the system response follows oral and written reminders, as opposed to warnings. It is a time for employees to think through the situation, and commit themselves to the improvement. The worker has leave for one day on full pay.

The planned and organized nature of the coaching intervention means that it is not just the same as a casual discussion. And decision-making leave is a serious matter, not a holiday. Karen and Bill are supervisors following the Discipline without Punishment approach.

Karen's approach

"When I coach an under-performing worker, I really have researched thoroughly. I know what's wrong, and I work hard to get the worker's agreement."

Bill's approach

"For a worker to return to his job after decision-making leave, he has to show commitment. He must actively decide to improve, and convince me of his determination."

Question

Problem Performance Management

Tony is a supervisor in a company that has recently adopted the Discipline without Punishment approach. He has to tell his team members about the distinctive and unique attributes of the system. Which statements identify those attributes?

Options:

1. The supervisor has to coach the problem employee in a planned discussion, with the goal of improving performance.

2. Coaching should be a spontaneous and casual discussion between the supervisor and employee.

3. Decision-making leave is to enable employees to commit themselves to an improvement in performance.

4. Decision-making leave is an opportunity for employees to have a break from work, and to come back refreshed.

Answer

Actually, the unique features of the system are a planned coaching session, designed to improve performance, and decision-making leave, which gives employees the time to fully commit themselves to improvement.

Option 1: Correct. The supervisor needs to clarify his performance expectations. His coaching session needs to end with the employee agreeing to make a positive change in his behavior.

Option 2: Incorrect. Proper coaching requires sufficient preparation and planning. A casual discussion may send mixed messages about your intent.

Option 3: Correct. Decision-making leave is a one day leave with pay that allows the employee to consider her situation and choose to commit herself to an acceptable level of performance.

Option 4: Incorrect. An employee is expected to use this leave to ponder on how he can meet his job expectations--and come back to work recommitted.

Discipline without Punishment requires managers and supervisors to apply the coaching sessions, and the decision-making leave opportunities most purposefully, and appropriately.

Coaching

You must identify the difference between actual and desired performance. Gain full agreement from the worker to the change by listing the business reasons for improvement and the consequences of lack of improvement. Then you can reiterate the action the worker will take.

Decision-making leave

You must explain the purpose of the leave to the worker, and confirm that it is a last opportunity before termination is considered. Workers must decide whether they will fully commit themselves to improvement or quit and find alternative employment.

The Discipline without Punishment approach is based on getting workers to take responsibility for the changes to maintain performance standards. This means that Jim must have his actual performance compared with the performance expected of him. And he must agree that it is his responsibility to make the changes, and confirm that he will do so. Then, if his behavior does not improve, he is going against this agreement.

Case Study: Question 1 of 2
Scenario

Problem Performance Management

Erica ignored the request of a manager to help two other employees with a complicated order. She told the manager, who was not from her department, that he was not her boss, and couldn't tell her what to do. She then carried on with the task she had been assigned by her immediate supervisor. You are going to give Erica some coaching about her performance.

Answer these questions, in order, to show how you should proceed.

Question

You call Erica into your office. Which statements would be appropriate when you are giving her coaching in the Discipline without Punishment system?

Options:

1. "You disobeyed the order of a manager."

2. "Our policy is that employees will follow instructions from any manager. You refused to do that."

3. "I want your agreement that you will always follow the instructions of any manager in the company."

4. "Don't ever do that again. Okay?"

5. "You must accept orders from any manager. If workers choose who they obey, the authority of all managers will be jeopardized. And you will be identified as a problem worker by all managers in the company."

Answer

Actually, in coaching Erica, you should identify the difference between actual and desired performance. You should get an agreement to the change by listing the business reasons for improvement, and the consequences of lack of improvement.

Option 1: Incorrect. Erica will not be able to use this statement to determine the nature of the problem, the effects of her behavior, or the behavior that is expected of her.

Option 2: Correct. This statement clearly explains Erica's infraction, and relates how her behavior contradicts company policies.

Option 3: Correct. This clearly outlines your performance expectations for Erica, as well as your expectation that she will agree with your requirements. She can use this information to judge her future behavior.

Option 4: Incorrect. The expectations for Erica's performance have not been clearly explained. She can only assume that she is supposed to act in a certain way.

Option 5: Correct. This outlines what may result from Erica's poor behavior. The statement also restates the level of performance that Erica is expected to maintain.

Case Study: Question 2 of 2

Erica, in spite of making an agreement to change her behavior, repeats her unwillingness to obey orders from managers outside her department. You give her formal reminders, but this does not change matters. You decide to give her decision-making leave. How will you go about explaining this to her?

Options:

1. "Erica, you agreed that you would obey all managers. Now you must decide whether you can really honor that commitment. I'm putting you on decision-making leave to let you think about your decision."

2. "Erica, you agreed to obey orders, but you haven't. I'm going to have to put you on immediate decision-making leave."

3. "Erica, we can't tolerate this behavior. Decision-making leave will show you that."

Problem Performance Management

4. "Erica, this is your last chance to make such a commitment, and honor it. If you can't, you'd better get another job."

Answer

In fact, you must explain the purpose of the leave, and confirm that it is a last opportunity. Workers must decide whether they will fully commit themselves to improvement, or quit and find alternative employment.

Option 1: Correct. You have explained to Erica the reason why she is being put on decision-making leave, as well as explained your expectation of her during this leave.

Option 2: Incorrect. This statement doesn't explain the purpose of the leave. That leaves room for misinterpretation on Erica's part.

Option 3: Incorrect. You have not explained to Erica how you expect her to use her leave. It is important that Erica not feel like she is just getting the day off.

Option 4: Correct. This statement outlines the actions that you must take if Erica's behavior does not improve. She now knows that dismissal may be the next step, and she can modify her behavior however she chooses.

When handling Erica using the Discipline without Punishment system, you have to explain to her the difference between her actual, and desired performance, and get her agreement to change her ways. This agreement gives you a tool to use if she does not improve.

Then, as a final chance, you can put her on decision-making leave to confirm her commitment to the agreement to change and return to work. Alternatively, if she decides not to commit, allow her to resign and look for alternative employment or fire her.

Discipline without Punishment will not be the right approach for every company. But now you have a working knowledge of the approach to help you make an informed choice about whether to follow this system.

www.ingramcontent.com/pod-product-compliance
Lightning Source LLC
Chambersburg PA
CBHW031607210526
45464CB00004B/1471